HERBAL ALCHEMY

Phillip Hurley

Revised edition,
Leigh Hurley, ed.

MAITHUNA PUBLICATIONS
Wheelock, Vermont

Copyright ©1977, ©2001 Phillip Hurley

All rights reserved. Except for properly attributed brief quotations for the purpose of critical review, this book may not be reproduced in whole or in part, in any form or by any means electronic or mechanical, including photocopying, recording, or by any information retrieval system now known or hereafter invented, without written permission from the author.

Original edition published 1977
  Lotus Publications, Chicago, Illinois

Revised edtion published 2001
  Maithuna Publications, Wheelock, Vermont

Notice

This book is intended as a reference volume only, not as a medical manual or guide to self-treatment. The author cautions you not to attempt diagnosis or embark on self-treatment of serious illness without competent professional assistance. The information presented in this book is not intended to substitute for any treatment that may have been prescribed by your physician.

Cover Illustration, Cover and Book Design by Leigh Hurley
Illustrations by Kasia Lynch and Leigh Hurley

Published by Maithuna Publications, an imprint of
  Good Idea Creative Services
  324 Minister Hill Road
  Wheelock Vermont 05851

ISBN 0-9710125-0-4

Library of Congress Control Number: 2001117030

Table of Contents

Introduction 1
On the Nature of the Five Elements 7
Hermetic Philosophy, Theory and Practice........ 12
Meditation on the Circle Point Mandala 20
Elemental Transmutation........................ 23
Astrology and Alchemy 27
Planetary Principles, their Analogies and Virtues
in the Vegetable Kingdom 32
    The Moon 33
        Lunar Plants in Application 35
    The Sun 37
        Solar Plants in Application 38
    Mercury 39
        Plants of Mercury in Application 41
    Venus 43
        Plants of Venus in Application............... 44
    Mars 47
        Plants of Mars in Application 48
    Jupiter..................................... 50
        Plants of Jupiter in Application 51
    Saturn..................................... 53
        Plants of Saturn in Application 56

Table of Contents

Uranus 58
   Plants of Uranus in Application. 59
Neptune 60
   Plants of Neptune in Application 62
Pluto. 65
Collection and Preparation of Plants 66
The Alchemist's Laboratory. 69
Salt, Sulphur and Mercury. 72
Preparing the Menstruum. 73
Extracting the Herbal Elixir 76
Medicinal Use of the Elixirs 80
Magical Impregnation of the Elixirs 82
Quabbalistic Values for the Planetary Spheres. 93
  Yesod, the Sphere of the Moon 95
  Tiphareth, the Sphere of the Sun. 96
  Hod, the Sphere of Mercury. 97
  Netzach, the Sphere of Venus 98
  Geburah, the Sphere of Mars 99
  Chesed, the Sphere of Jupiter. 100
  Binah, the Sphere of Saturn 101
Solve et Coagula. 102
Resources for Further Study 104

Introduction

Alchemy is an ancient spiritual practice and art, understood by very few people throughout its long history. This is still true in the modern world. Most contemporary works on the subject are mere historical sketches of what is regarded as an arcane science. From an Alchemist's point of view, this is unfortunate, because Alchemy is very much alive and thriving, more so now than ever before.

The old alchemical assertion that it is possible to change one element into another was widely ridiculed. But now, on a daily basis scientists perform such transmutations in their laboratories, turning one element into another with high powered accelerators. Other scientists are working to unlock the secrets of low temperature- low energy transmutation, a process which the Alchemists of old said was possible. The advent of quantum physics has brought forth startling revelations about the connection between consciousness and matter, and the effect of the observer on the observed. In this new light, old inscrutable alchemical axioms that once seemed nonsense can now be understood; and the essence of alchemical doctrine is actually becoming part of the mainstream spiritual- scientific thought of our times.

What is Alchemy? The origin of the name itself is somewhat obscure, but it is generally thought to be an ancient reference to Egypt. Egypt was called the land of *Chem* or *Cham*, meaning "land of black earth," which in Alchemy also refers to *prima materia* (first matter). *Al* or *El* refers to the prime source, infinite spirit or absolute. So, "Alchemy" refers to the art itself, and to its origins in ancient Egypt.

Herbal Alchemy

India and China both also have long traditions of Alchemy. In India, the legends of the Tantric Alchemists Kankanapa and Nagarjuna are the basis for the story of the radiant jewel in the lotus, which in turn is the origin of the famous Vajrayana mantra *Om Mani Padme Hum.*

The jewel within the lotus is called the three-fold jewel (*tri-ratma*), about which legend states, "He who possesses this jewel overcomes death and rebirth and gains immortality and liberation." The jewel itself is the same as the Philosophers Stone of the Alchemists, and it is no coincidence that the Egyptians referred to Toth as "thrice great," and the Greeks referred to Hermes similarly, as *Trismegistus.*

It is also no coincidence that the vajra of Indra is one of the most important symbols for Tantrics. The vajra is Indra's power or magical tool, and in the Tantric tradition it is symbolic of the highest spiritual power. These philosophies arose directly from Vedic culture and its associated yogas, as did most of the later Taoist and Buddhist alchemical traditions.

Through whatever tradition the science of Alchemy is studied, it should become apparent that Alchemy applies to organic forms of life as well as what is considered inorganic; and to what is considered the "immaterial" as well as the "material." From the Alchemist's point of view, everything has consciousness; thus distinctions such as organic and inorganic, or material and immaterial, fade one into the other.

Put very simply, Alchemy is the science of "the Source," the universal spirit, the absolute. This source is considered the Grand Alchemist, and its body or manifestation in all dimensions is its laboratory or realm of being – our universe.

Very few people are aware of the profundity and breadth of the alchemical path. To be an Alchemist, one must be all at

Introduction

once a mystic, a magician, and a scientist. Intuition, intellect and action are smoothly integrated, each of them informing the others. In the Alchemist's unending quest for knowledge, all aspects of existence are proper subjects for meditation, experimentation and analysis. William Blake put it well, "The true method of knowledge is experiment. All of life for us is experiment and discovery," and again in the words of Blake, "To see a world in a grain of sand, And a heaven in a wild-flower, hold infinity in the palm of your hand, and eternity in an hour."

The goal of the Alchemist is to center themself within the consciousness of the ultimate creative principle, so that they can understand the universe in all its diversity as one great process. Alchemical tradition states that from this center of creative consciousness, all can be comprehended and experienced. This point of centering is the esoteric Philosophers Stone, and is the understanding diverse spiritual disciplines express with such terms as cosmic consciousness, satori, enlightenment, and so forth. The Alchemist derives knowledge from this center of creative consciousness – and it resides within the Alchemist themself.

In all spiritual disciplines, the key to understanding the nature of the universe, the secret of the Philosophers Stone, is contained within. For example, in the Tantric tradition the *mani* or Philosophers Stone lies in the *padma*, the lotus of the heart. All Yoga systems refer every question and answer back to the self. In Tantric Yoga this is stated quite aptly in the mantra *Aum Aham Brahma Smi*, meaning, "I am the creator."

So, the beginning of the quest for the Philosophers Stone is an inner journey which requires a study of oneself and the development of intuition. The Alchemist must learn to feel mystically the principles worked with, remembering the hermetic axiom, *"as above so below, as within so without."* This requires many years of consistent practice of the art of meditation. The prime meditation during these years is on the Philosophers Stone, the center of universal consciousness, the creative spark.

The next step is for the Alchemist to transfer this mystical feeling into knowledge, which usually takes place as one progresses in the practice of meditation. This process of transformation, that is, transmuting intuition into knowledge, is the attainment of magical knowledge or what is referred to in the East as *siddhi* (the power that comes from knowing).

The completion of this process, for lack of a better word, we will call meta-scientific. It is the direct linking up of mystical feeling and magical knowledge to dense substance or physical plane material. In other words, the intuitive feeling of the mystical experience is translated into an intellectual knowing, which informs action, affecting the materia of all three planes – physical, mental, and astral.

Essentially the Alchemist operates as a magician and a mystic, and can also produce the same metaphysical cause and effect phenomena through physical plane disciplines. They seek not only to discover the universal consciousness within, but then proceed to translate this knowledge into active expression, and with this cosmic creativity, transform themselves and the world around them. So, in addition to studying the techniques of magic and mysticism, the Alchemist is a student of the techniques of their own chosen physical plane pursuits, whether arts or science, but not limited to these mundane categories. The Alchemist's access to the knowledge and inspiration of the Philosophers Stone makes their work, whether art, craft or science, "come

Introduction

alive." For indeed, every human endeavor, every movement in time and space has its source and its affects, and is a possible subject for the Alchemist's meditation and experimentation. All life is cosmic art to the Alchemist.

The Alchemist can perceive in the operation of an atomic or molecular structure, a part of the mystical body of the ultimate source, or a blade of grass and the song of a bird – and in any of these things, the others. It is a continuity of consciousness so profound that words cannot describe it.

In this work on the lesser arcanum of Alchemy, we will deal with the three modes of alchemical expression as a whole in the context of the art of Herbal Alchemy. This represents only a small part of the scope of Alchemy, but it is hoped that even those who do not have an affinity for working with the plant world will be able to learn something useful about the art of Alchemy that can be applied to their own fields of interest. The intent of this book is not to provide recipes, but to give people a starting point for working with alchemical techniques. Truly, the whole point of Alchemy is to NOT be a slave to any book or formula, but to meditate, experiment and analyze, and come to one's own conclusions.

Today quantum physics tells us that all matter and its actions are affected by the observer. This is why the magical ritual method included in this work is of prime importance and should not be taken lightly.

Finally, the Alchemist understands that Alchemy is not owned by any philosophical-theological group or religion. Again, the words of William Blake will help the student to understand that while researching alchemical literature, one should skim the overlay and look deeper for the essence of the work:

Herbal Alchemy

The ancient Poets animated all sensible objects
with Gods or Geniuses,

Calling them by the names and adorning them

With the properties of woods, rivers, mountains,
lakes, cities, nations,

And whatever their enlarged & numerous
senses could perceive.

And particularly they studied the genius of each city
and country, placing it under its mental deity.

Till a system was formed,
which some took advantage of

And enslaved the vulgar by attempting to realize
or abstract the mental deities from their objects;

Thus began Priesthood, choosing
forms of worship from Poetic tales.

And at length they announced
that the Gods had ordered such things

Thus men forgot
that all deities reside in the human breast.

William Blake (1757-1827)

To be an Alchemist, you must realize that you are the beginning and end of all things, and the interplay in between. No one can give you this knowledge but yourself; no one can give you enlightenment but yourself.

On the Nature of the Five Elements

According to the Alchemists, all manifestation on all planes of existence (dimensions of time and space) are composed of five elements. It is the action of these elements and their relationships with each other that produce the myriad of manifestation surrounding us. The first element, from which all others are derived, is called the Akasha Principle.

Akasha is a Sanskrit term, similar to the Western concept of ether. This substance is the universal matrix from which, and within which, all phenomena occur. It contains within it the infinity of all possibilities. The Akasha Principle or etheric substrate is the quintessence for the Alchemist. Sometimes called the fifth power, it contains within it the other four elements and all their interactions. It is the prima materia of the universe – the ultimate source of all manifestation.

From the one (akasha) arise the four elements – Fire, Air, Earth, and Water. It should be understood that although these elements have a strong affinity for the physical fire, air, earth, and water, the subtle elements and their gross physical representations are not the same thing. In fact, physical matter is exceedingly complex combinations of these principles, because of the almost limitless possibilities of combinations.

On the physical plane these forces are the building blocks of matter. It is now widely accepted that what seems solid to us – physical matter – consists of a variety of sub-atomic particles and wavelike structures that are, on one level, simply electromagnetic fields, acting and interacting with one another. At matter's most fundamental levels, the "real" and "solid" is actually just electrically charged empty space.

Today scientists are more confused than ever by the nature of matter, as they are discovering that at subatomic levels, matter behaves very strangely indeed.

According to the Alchemists, the key to understanding our universe is meditation, and the study and observation of the four elements as they manifest before us. The elements have analogs on our physical plane. When the physical counterparts are meditated upon, they can connect us with their first principles and bring us to a better understanding of them. This works a little like current quantum string theory which posits that there are subtle connections inter-dimensionally between various materia and their essential natures.

It should be stated that "to understand" means "to meditate upon" in alchemical terms. In Alchemy, the study of anything requires meditation as well as physically working with the various principles in manifestation. The Alchemist's meditation is both esoteric (inward) and exoteric (outward). The "inward" and "outward" come together in what Zen practitioners would call *satori* or enlightenment.

This may seem an unusual mode of learning to the Western mind, which is devoted to outward observation and does not see much merit in developing intuitive observation. However, from the Alchemist's perspective, it's hard to understand why anyone would not want to use both their right and left brain in any pursuit. Indeed, the most important function of the alchemical process is the development of the Alchemist's intuitive faculties through meditation, and training the intellect (left brain) to be informed by the intuition (right brain).

On the Nature of the Five Elements

A good example of this process can be found in the practices of Tantric Alchemists. For instance, to understand and develop a working knowledge of the Akasha Principle they would simply meditate upon the syllable *ham* (the seed syllable for Akasha). This can be done by first repeating the mantra *ham* continuously over and over until the connection is felt. Once the connection is established, the Alchemist continues on a daily basis to work with the mantra and meditation. Over time the Alchemist develops more and more of a feel for the nature of the Akasha vibration, and slowly the knowledge contained within that vibration becomes more readily accessible to them.

To further their study, the Tantric Alchemist meditates upon the other four elements using the seed syllable for each element as a guide. Each sound has a vibratory rate with an affinity for its corresponding element. For Fire, the Tantric will meditate on the seed syllable *ram*; for Air, it would be *yam*; for Water, *vam*; and for Earth, *lam*. While meditating on the nature of each these forces, the Tantric imagines the attributes of the element contemplated. Meditation upon the Fire element is accompanied by a visualization of the color red and an imagined sensation of heat; for the element of Water, the color green and a sense of coolness; for Air, a sensation of lightness and the visualization of the color light blue; and for the Earth element the visualization is the color yellow-ochre and a sense of heaviness. These meditations lead to understanding and knowledge that is referred to as *siddhis* or powers. There are many stories of Tantric yogis who are capable of producing great amounts of heat from their bodies as in the practice of *tumo* in Tibet, which involves meditation on the element of Fire; and in

India, of Tantrics levitating themselves through a meditation upon the element of Air.

These may seem like fairy tales, but hidden within each of us are capabilities beyond our dreams. Within each of us is the knowledge of all things. To the Alchemist, life's work is to recognize this intuitive part of the self and develop an ongoing dialogue. This is truly the beginning of great understanding and gives the Alchemist the keys to unlock the mysteries of the universe.

This concept of dialogue was understood by the ancients. They assigned various anthropomorphic forms (deities and angels, spirits etc.) to cosmic forces to create a kind of perceptual handle for people. A familiar form that could speak and seem almost human provided a comfort factor so that a bridge could be formed between the energy involved and the seeker of knowledge.

As humans, we are actually bundles of electromagnetic forces that interact with other bundles of electromagnetic forces. However, we think of these forces in anthropomorphic terms – character, personality – rather than describe ourselves in the terms of physics. It is not difficult to understand why humans tend to do the same for other types of bundled forces. It really does not matter exactly how we choose to perceive the universe – but it is important that we recognize that our conventional frames of reference are limited structures. They are shaped by our personal karma, and the karma of an epoch or historical period, and thus severely constrained. The Alchemist must learn to open up their perceptions beyond such restrictions.

The operation of the five elements and the practice of Alchemy encompasses the whole of life. From any level of

On the Nature of the Five Elements

understanding, the whole of nature is an interplay between the elemental forces. There are many compartmentalized ranges of study and specialization within the scope of Alchemy. But, in the broadest sense, it is an attitude born of the endeavor to balance the nature of the elements within ourselves. This has impact outwardly as well as inwardly, as we become walking-talking representations of the Philosophers Stone.

One can be an Alchemist and study the nature of the five elements at any octave. For instance, someone who has a propensity for psychology can study and apply alchemical principles to that particular discipline. The application of the alchemical understanding of the elements will enrich the pursuit of any discipline. Alchemy has much more to do with life in its entirety than simply transmuting lead to gold on the physical plane. Lead to gold means much more than that.

Each person has a contribution to make with the particular combination of elemental forces which comprise their own unique personalities. The experiences of life itself give each of us transmutory power – a bit of the Philosophers Stone, if you will, and those whom we touch with our knowledge and experience are forever transformed whether we realize it or not. Each interaction creates a new level of awareness that brings us closer to the source. All of life is essentially an alchemical process of transformation and transmutation – and an adventure and journey of discovery. In this small book we deal specifically with the application of alchemical theory and the operation of the elements within the plant kingdom. However, the real purpose of this book is to help the reader to recognize their own potential and apply these principles in the spheres where their particular talent lies.

Hermetic Philosophy, Theory and Practice

Each major spiritual discipline has a magical glyph which creatively synthesizes its philosophy. For Alchemy, the major initiation diagrams are the symbol of the planet Mercury, the Caduceus of Hermes, and the simple circle-point mandala. Each of these, though visually different, represents the same philosophical concepts. They are drawn differently according to octave of use. To comprehend these symbols is to understand the entire creative process of Alchemy.

Our first consideration is the circle-point mandala. According to alchemical lore, the universe first manifested itself as the universal creative spark. For an analogy, this can be considered an electrical charge. Simultaneously, a magnetic field of 360 degrees was created around the central spark. This universal magnetic field became the etheric substructure for all manifestation, and explains the old Alchemists' axiom that all things were created simultaneously. Physicists know that with every electrical charge you must have a surrounding magnetic field. If you remove either the electrical charge or the magnetic field, the other collapses. Thus in saying that everything was created at once, the old Alchemists meant that the archetypal manifestations of all objects, thoughts, and types of interactions between them were created instantly due to lines of magnetic stress. This divine creative spark is the energy and form-giver of our universe. Everything that we can perceive is the result of the ideation of this universal spark.

Hermetic Philosophy, Theory and Practice

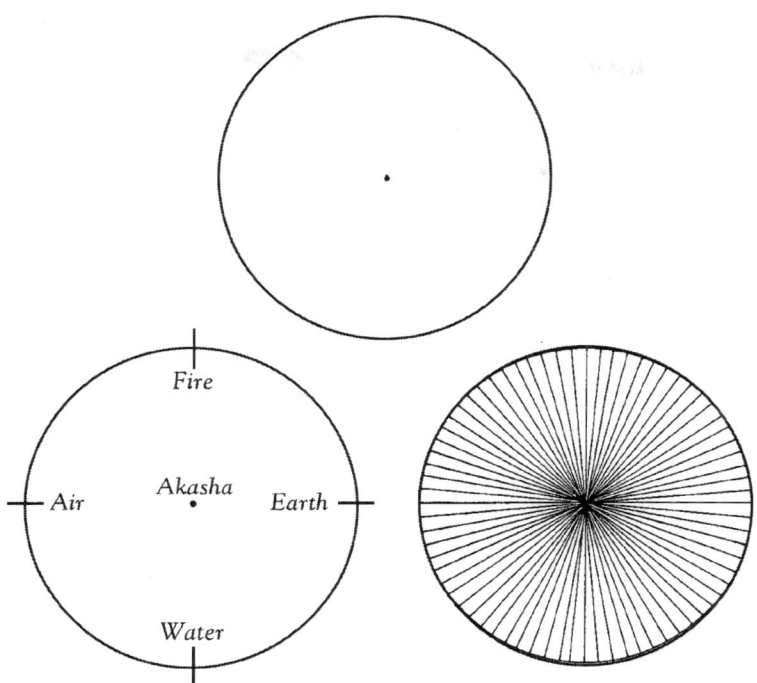

Three versions of the circle point mandala

There is another old alchemical riddle which puzzles many, but can be readily understood when the relevant alchemical analogies are applied. It is: "How does the Creator who is one become five yet remain one?" The answer to this riddle is that every electromagnetic field (the one) has its polarities, that is, a north and south pole. These two polarities were called the elements of Fire and Water by the ancient Alchemists. At the quarter points, on each side of these fields are two more polarities, or what the Alchemists call the mediating elements of Air and Earth. What we have now is the universal quadripolar magnet. This is the tetragrammaton of the ancient Alchemists, the IHVH of the Quabbalists, and is symbolically represented by the solar cross. The creative spark in the center is the fifth element,

Herbal Alchemy

The Caduceus of Hermes

Akasha. So it is easy to see by analogy how the universal spark which is one becomes five yet remains one.

The next alchemical symbol to be studied is the glyph of the Caduceus of Hermes. The caduceus is not only a diagram of the human spinal system, but also represents the spinal evolutionary makeup of the universe. The caduceus is merely the circle point mandala in extension, formed by overlapping two sine curves (usually represented by two intertwining serpents) along a vertical axis. This represents what the Tantrics call the *ida*, *pingala* and *sushumna* channels of the spiritual spinal system on all planes of existence. At each crossing of the double sine curve on the *bindu* point is what is called a chakra, sephira, etc. depending on what system you adhere to. This chakra system occurs not only in

Hermetic Philosophy, Theory and Practice

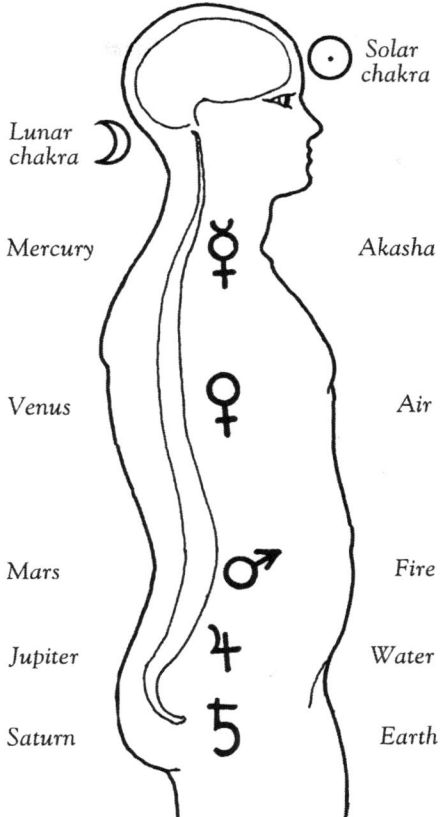

The Human Chakra System

humans, but our solar system also has these centers which we call planets. (For that matter, everything else that exists also has a chakra system).

At the lowest point in the human spinal system, at the coccyx, is the Saturn chakra. The next planetary center is at the point on the spine at the small of the back. This is the Jupiter chakra. The Mars chakra is on the spine at the level of the navel. The Venus chakra is at about heart level on the spine. The Mercury chakra is at the back of the neck on the spine. The Sun and Moon chakras are actually one chakra, but are considered two from the human perspective of looking up from the planes of duality as we do. The Sun is at the point between the eyebrows and the Moon behind the head at the soft part of the skull, just above the Mercury chakra.

The Glyph of Mercury

The thousand petaled lotus is above the head and comes into existence for us when we synthesize the polarity of Sun and Moon and cease to be torn between them. When the solar and lunar forces in our being are balanced by centering ourselves we are no longer victimized by the karmic nature of the grand interplay between Fire and Water. On a personal level this is the experience of cosmic consciousness. On the cosmic physical level this is considered the perfect state of balance.

The Alchemist will notice that Saturn, which rules lead, is at the bottom of the spine; and the Sun, which rules gold, is at the top. From this diagram one can understand why the major meditation in the discipline of yoga is the lifting of the *kundalini* up the spine from Saturn to Sun. The alchemical connection is quite obvious, as every book on Alchemy mentions the transmutation of lead into gold. The study of this glyph will give the knowledge necessary to carry out physical as well as spiritual transformation.

The third glyph to be considered is the astrological symbol for the planet Mercury. This diagram is the same as the caduceus. The crescent represents the *ida* channel, the circle *sushumna*, and the cross represents the *pingala*.

Hermetic Philosophy, Theory and Practice

These last two glyphs referred to, Mercury and the caduceus, are composed of three philosophical principles. The mythological father of this triadic philosophy is Hermes Trismegistus ("Thrice Great Hermes") from whom this art (Hermetics) takes its name. The essence of his philosophy was said to have been engraved on an emerald tablet. This is one version of what was written on that tablet:

1. True without falsehood, certain and most true, that which is above is the same as that which is below, and that which is without is the same as that which is within, for the performance of the miracles of the one thing. And as all things are from one, by the mediation of one, so all things have their birth from this one thing by adaptation.

2. The Sun is its father, the Moon its mother, the Wind carries it in its belly and the Earth is its nurse and guardian. This is the father of all perfection or consummation of the whole world

3. Its power is integrating if it be turned into Earth. You shall separate the Earth from the Fire, the subtle from the gross, suavely and with great ingenuity and skill. Your skillful work ascends from Earth and descends to Earth, and receives the powers of the superiors and of the inferiors.

So you have the glory of the whole world. Therefore let all obscurity flee before you. This is the strong force of all forces, overcoming every subtle and penetrating every solid thing.

So the world was created. Hence were all wonderful adaptations of which this is the manner. Therefore am I called Hermes Trismegistus, having the three parts of the philosophy of the whole world. What I have to tell is completed concerning the operation of the Sun.

Herbal Alchemy

This philosophical statement is the cornerstone of all magical philosophy. It can be applied to discern the secret operation of the occult forces of nature. To the esoteric student, each word has its rulership in an astrological and an elemental sense, and from this comes the knowledge of the meaning of the occult message within.

Hermes begins his exposition by speaking of truth. This opening line gives the apprentice the secret key that unlocks the door to the Hermetic sciences. "True without falsehood, certain and most true," indicates that truth is the major symbol and tool of this art. Truth is ruled by the planet Mercury, whose symbol is the caduceus which is a representation of the spinal column.

He then proceeds, "that which is above is the same as that which is below, and that which is without is the same as that which is within for the performance of the miracles of the one thing. " Here he is stating a most profound space-time concept which is the foundation of all practical magic. The Alchemist with some background in Zen technique will instantly recognize the similarity between this statement and the koans of the Zen tradition. From the dawn of the human search, statements like those of Hermes, which are in essence koans, have been used to bring the initiate to an enlightened understanding of universal processes. To the uninitiated these koans are nonsense, but for those who have entered the temple of the mysteries, they are a profound statement of universal law. In essence Hermes has stated that although there is an apparent distinction between objects in this universe, they are all one, and that they occupy the same space-time location. This means literally that everything is contained within everything else. This concept is the basis for the true understanding of the operation of all of the arts of divination.

Hermetic Philosophy, Theory and Practice

Hermes continues by saying "The Sun is its father, the Moon its mother. The Wind carries it in its belly and the Earth is its nurse and guardian. This is the father of all perfection, or consummation of the whole world." Here he is simply stating that the etheric substrate Akasha divides itself into four main polarities as discussed in reference to the circle-point mandala. The Sun here represents the element of Fire, and the Moon the element of Water. Hermes ends part two by saying that this knowledge is, "The father of perfection or consummation of the whole world," that is, by and through the action of these four elements all is created, sustained and dissolved.

Part three is a more direct statement indicating the actual process of transmutation and in general, the occult key to the mastery of the operation of the tetragrammaton. Here he says, "Its power is integrating if it be turned into Earth. You shall separate the Earth from the Fire, the subtle from the gross, suavely and with great ingenuity and skill. Your skillful work ascends from Earth to Heaven and descends again to Earth and receives the powers of the superiors and the inferiors." This last and most important section will be discussed in the chapter on elemental transmutation, which is an operational precise of the above statement.

Practice
Meditation on the Circle Point Mandala

The circle-point mandala is the Alchemist's doorway to universal consciousness or knowledge of the Philosophers Stone. The term universe means one-verse. That simple center point within the mandala is the "one-verse" which Tantrics vocalize as the seed syllable *Aum* and Quabbalists as *Eheiah*. The circle represents all of manifestation derived from the center point or source. Visual renditions of this universal creative matrix are called *yantras* and *mandalas* in the Far East. In the Western magical tradition, the magician

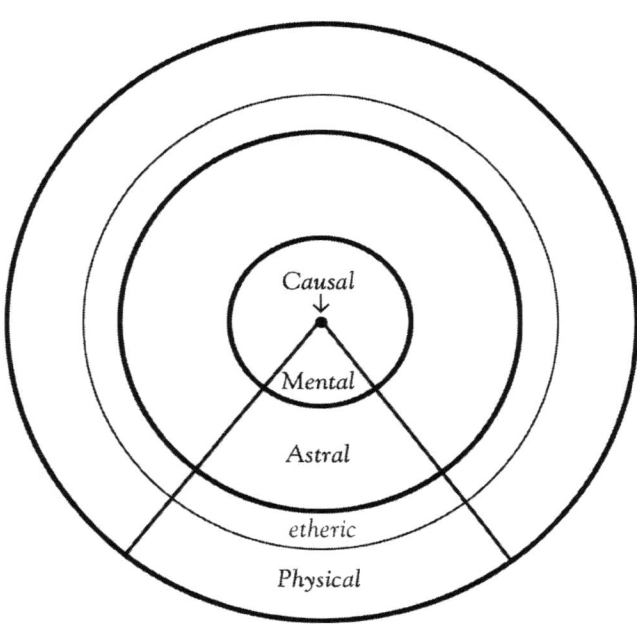

The planes of existence shown on the Circle-Point Mandala

Meditation on the Circle Point Mandala

draws a circle-mandala upon the ground and steps into the center of the circle to connect with universal consciousness.

To construct this mandala, purchase a good sturdy piece of art board about three feet by three feet. Upon this, draw the circle in yellow and the point in violet. The size of the circle and the center point should be proportioned to your aesthetic tastes. Set up the mandala in a place set aside specifically for meditation. Two candles should be set up on either side of the mandala.

In preparation for the first meditation, perform a ritual bath to eliminate and wash away any inharmonious elements within your etheric-physical body. At the same time, realize that you are eliminating inharmonious vibrations from your astral and mental bodies through the cleansing action of the physical water. While performing this ritual bath, see to it that you are not disturbed so that your thoughts remain entirely on the universal consciousness you seek.

After the cleansing ritual, light the candles on either side of the mandala and sit about four feet away facing the mandala. Focus your eyes on the center point, and realize that this is the consciousness of the essence. As you gaze into the center, feel that this presence is located within this point. When by intuition you feel its presence in the mandala, close your eyes and feel the radiance emanating from this point towards and through you, and feel it raising your vibratory rate at all levels. This should result in a complete sense of harmony and balance, best described as a state of bliss.

During your meditations, let yourself feel this presence physically, emotionally and mentally; in other words, maintain full concentration on it in the mental, astral and physical body. After a reasonable amount of time, end the meditation by ritually bowing before the mandala in recognition of the presence of the universal essence. Extinguish the candles and cover the mandala with a silk drape. Remember that this is your doorway to link with the universal essence, so it should not be used for any other purpose. Otherwise, all your meditations will have been for nothing as the vibration will be transformed with other concerns that will dilute the experience.

These meditations should begin on the day of the New Moon and continued every day for about 28 days, in other words, until the time of the next New Moon. If at all possible, begin your meditations at the New Moon that first precedes or follows the Vernal Equinox (whichever one is closer).

At the time of the next New Moon, proceed as before, except that now, you will combine your consciousness with that of the universal essence. Before this union takes place, you should eat lightly or fast for at least one day before hand. During this preparation period, ponder the event that is to take place. On the New Moon, sit facing the mandala, and meditate upon the universal emanation, but now after you close your eyes, project your own consciousness into the center point and link your consciousness to the creative essence. You should feel this merging as an ecstasy and should stay centered there as long as you like.

When finished, bring your consciousness back to your body, and as you do, realize that a part of the universal consciousness comes back with you. In Alchemy this union is called the mystical marriage and will have profound effects on your life. Remember to remain passively receptive to the influx of the universal essence during your meditations, and fix your attention on this only. This meditation should be practiced daily, if possible.

Elemental Transmutation

One of the most deeply hidden aspects of Alchemy is the process of creating and dissolving matter. What follows here has been up to this time an extremely well kept secret. As far as the author is aware, this book is the first time that this process has been given out in such an easily understood format. In essence what is here is the practical key to the use of the tetragrammaton.

Although it is important to have a theoretical and historical knowledge of Alchemy, all this is of no use if the practitioner does not possess the means to produce and realize, first hand, the operations of nature. Once realizing the truth by practical application, the apprentice Alchemist will no longer have any doubts about whether they are following a true path with some substance, or whether or not they are merely deluding themselves with a wishful fantasy. There are many formulas of elemental transmutation in use, but here, the key will be given to the Tantric formula. In the author's experience, it has been found to be more directly effective and dynamic as far as immediate results are concerned, and is very good for those who do not have much prior practice with meditation.

As mentioned earlier, there are various centers situated on the spine. These centers are in essence step up and step down transformers, as well as centers of radiation for a specific type of energy. In different systems of initiation these centers are placed in different locations in the body. The varying placement of these centers in different systems should not confuse you as the idea behind them is the same throughout every mystery school.

Herbal Alchemy

In this Tantric mantra cycle, the energy is drawn through the Sun center and down through each successive center until the thought is earthed in the last one. Each of these centers steps down the spiritual energy to a lower vibratory rate causing a stabilization or concretizing of that thought into a specific form which physicists call matter. What is actually occurring is a most profound process. The Alchemist is actually arranging atoms and molecules of substance directly from spirit, which is no small feat. The creation of matter from the Alchemist's own causal impetus is a truly satisfying experience for the beginning apprentice.

In the system presented here, each center has a simple seed syllable mantra which unlocks the door to each transformer and lowers the vibratory rate of the thought patterns that we wish to materialize.

The seed syllables are as follows:

AUM	Sun Center
HA	Akasha
YA	Air
RA	Fire
VA	Water
LA	Earth

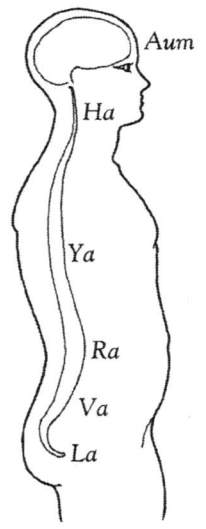

Location of the seed syllables

Before using this technique, memorize the seed syllable mantras by heart. After memorizing them to the point that there is no doubt in mind as to their order and progression, proceed to learn their proper placement

Elemental Transmutation

and sequence along the spine. This is practiced by running up and down the spine mentally pronouncing each seed syllable in the appropriate chakra. When you are able to do this with ease and without hesitation, you are then ready for the practice of materialization.

When working with this technique it is best to face east during the day and north at night. The reason for this is that it helps to align your will with the geomagnetic flow of the earth sphere, and thus gives greater ease of working. After you sit down and position yourself facing the proper direction, you should relax and develop an attitude of calmness. For your first experiment, you should materialize such things as scents, for instance, rose oil, the scent of jasmine incense, etc. or some other scent that you are familiar with.

Once you have in mind the scent you wish to materialize you may proceed. Begin to draw energy into the Sun chakra mentally sounding the seed syllable *Aum*. Continue drawing this energy through to the Akasha chakra mentally sounding the seed syllable *Ha*, and so on down the line, pulling the energy all the way down to the Earth chakra and ending with the seed syllable *La*. While doing this, you must at the same time wish or desire that the scent you have chosen will materialize physically. It is very important to keep up your concentration on the scent that you want materialized while mentally pronouncing the seed syllables in each center as your thoughts descend and materialize on the Earth plane. After you reach the lowest center, start over again and keep repeating this process until you have succeeded. When you are satisfied that you have produced the desired result, reverse the process with the thought in mind that you are now dematerializing the scent you have made manifest. In other words you should start with the seed syllable *La* and proceed upwards to *Va*, and on through the rest finally to *Aum*.

Most everyone who practices this technique will have some measure of success and be able to produce such materialization phenomenon on the first try. If you have difficulty, stop and try again at a later time. You will notice sometimes the scent materializes in a thick layer, or it wafts; this is of course dependent on the nature of your abilities of concentration and other factors at the time.

At any rate, the purpose here is not to produce scents per se but to give the Alchemist a practical working magical tool with which they can prove to themselves the validity of transmutation, and provide an experimental start in the right direction to further understanding the hidden capabilities within us all. When you have successfully experienced this phenomenon, it will raise many questions for you, while at the same time providing many answers. This transmutation of energy to materia and vice versa is the operation of the tetragrammaton and is the operational equivalent of the $E = mc^2$ formula, wherein it states that matter can be transmuted to energy and energy transmuted into matter.

Astrology and Alchemy

The study of Astrology should go hand in hand with the study of Alchemy. Although it is not absolutely necessary, it is strongly advised as it will give the student a solid foundation for all esoteric studies. The base language of Alchemy is more often than not couched in astrological terms. In fact, the fundamental key to the secrets of Alchemy lies in the language and science of Astrology.

The term Astrology comes from astral logos meaning: "star logo" or "star law." Astral logos covers the nature, operation, and interactions of all materia in a time-space context – both what is considered organic and what is considered inorganic. This system helps us to discern the nature of fundamental principles within our solar system. It operates via the hermetic axiom "As above, so below; as within, so without."

The key to all processes and materia in our solar system is available to us through the study of Astrology. The knowledge and language of Astrology (Doctrine of Signatures) has been developed over thousands of years through observation by humans who noticed that certain celestial positions coincided with particular outward events, and with particular kinds of thoughts and feelings (inner events) within the consciousness.

The Doctrine of Signatures is based upon the fact that each object or event has the character (signature) of a planet, or particular combination of planets, which means that it vibrates (operates and responds) at a wavelength resonant with that planet or configuration. Each planet and/or com-

Herbal Alchemy

bination has an affinity or rulership with particular materia, at all levels, from micro to macro, and on all planes – astral and mental as well as physical. The Alchemist observes the planets and their cycles, and ascertains the nature of materia via the Doctrine of Signatures.

Astrology has nothing to do with "fate," as commonly perceived. It does describe the fundamental nature of matter on all planes, and matter's interactions within the context of our solar system. The nature of materia and its interactions are such that there are inharmonious (to our perceptions) and harmonious tendencies and results. This is totally relative – truly a matter of perception and position.

It can be said that Astrology provides us with a "weather report" of the actions of the four elements within our sphere of perception. These tendencies or flows in the cosmic tide affect us, but through alchemical transmutation or understanding according to our lights, these effects can be transformed. The creation of alchemical elixirs and the science of Feng Shui are two methods among many that allow us to transmute such energies and their flows. Meditation is another, and is a primary component of the alchemical path.

An astrological chart is actually a circle-point mandala. It reveals the intimate details of the configuration of forces at a particular moment and location on Earth. Such a chart can be very useful to the Alchemist for any manner of endeavor.

The Alchemist's meditation upon their own natal chart is an important part of alchemical study. A natal chart is calculated according to the time and place of a person's birth, and gives one a map of the forces involved in shaping a person's essential self as it manifests on this plane of existence.

Astrology & Alchemy

Alchemists use Astrology directly to choose auspicious times to begin various operations. This is discerned by studying the relationship between the Alchemist's natal chart, and the positions of the planets as they move in their orbits.

Certain operations are begun according to the day of the week, as each day is ruled by a planet. According to the Doctrine of Signatures, the Sun rules Sunday, the Moon rules Monday, Mars rules Tuesday, Mercury rules Wednesday, Jupiter rules Thursday, Venus rules Friday, and Saturn rules Saturday. Each of these days, according to esoteric cycles, has a vibration that is in concinnity with the planet mentioned for each day.

Even the hours of the day can be broken down according to these seven basic planets: at sunrise on any day begins the first planetary hour of the day, beginning with the planet that rules that day. For instance, Mercury would be the first planetary hour of Wednesday, and Jupiter, the first hour of Thursday. The period from sunrise to sunset is divided into twelve planetary hours, with the cycle continued in another twelve divisions from sunset to sunrise. The order of planets for the cycles of planetary hours would be: Saturn, Jupiter, Mars, Sun, Venus, Mercury, Moon.

There are many astrological texts on planetary hours and how to calculate them if one is interested. They have generally fallen into disuse. They can be of value in general applications – such as collecting herbs on certain days and hours – but usually Alchemists pay more attention to lunar cycles and planetary aspects than they do planetary hours and days.

Planetary aspects are the relationship between two or more planets at any given time. They are generally classed as harmonious or inharmonious according to the nature of the aspect. These aspects are usually given great significance in the timing of various alchemical operations. For those who are not acquainted with Astrology from a physical healing point of view, following is a small list of planetary attributes and characters that may be of interest or value.

Sun - the anterior pituitary gland, blood circulation, the heart and the arteries

Moon - the alimentary canal, female reproductive organs, the lymph glands, cerebellum, lower ganglia and sympathetic nervous system

Mercury and Uranus - the brain, and cerebrospinal nervous system.

Venus - the thymus gland, kidneys.

Mars - the cortical portion of the adrenal glands, and muscles.

Jupiter - the posterior pituitary gland, liver and blood plasma.

Saturn - parts of the adrenal glands, and the bones, teeth, joints and tendons and the spleen.

Uranus - the parathyroid gland, the brain and cerebral spinal system.

Neptune - the pineal gland

Pluto - the pancreas and digestive gland as well as the sexual organs.

These rulerships are important to determine what elixirs to use for problems related to certain organs. This is by no means a complete list and if one is interested in pursuing this area there are many books available that deal with medical astrology. There are also plenty of herbal manuals available that give specific herbs and their uses for ameliorating various physical dysfunctions. The Alchemist can apply any of these herbs according to these herbals but with alchemically prepared elixirs rather than with just tinctures or decoctions. Note as well that Ayurvedic preparations also rely heavily on astrological science for the preparation of their elixirs.

No matter what system or herbal planetary designations one uses, there are certain basic characteristics of each planet which are important to remember. The Sun, Mars, Jupiter, Uranus herbs are electric, yang and energizing, dominated by the Fire element; and the Moon, Venus, Saturn, Neptune and Pluto herbs are magnetic, yin and soothing, dominated by the Water element. These two elements, Fire and Water, are the original two elements of the Alchemists.

Planetary Principles, their Analogies and Virtues in the Vegetable Kingdom

Each initiating system has its own verbal designations for the seven planetary centers. The two most well known systems and their correspondences are given in the table below.

Planet	**Quabbala**	**Tantra Yoga**
Sun	Tiphareth	Ajna
Moon	Yesod	Chandra
Mercury	Hod	Vishuddha
Venus	Netzach	Anahata
Mars	Geburah	Manipura
Jupiter	Chesed	Svadhisthana
Saturn	Binah	Muladhara

Although the verbal designations are not the same, the force, form, function are. For instance, a Quabbalist meditating on *Tiphareth* would experience the same phenomenon that a yogi would meditating on the *Ajna* chakra, with only a slight difference due to built-up thought forms peculiar to each system. Some would disagree, to whom it should be said that with a lump of clay you can make a tea cup or a vase, but it's still the same lump of clay. Each system remolds the objective energies of each archetype to suit its own subjective transcendental ends.

Planetary Principles in the Vegetable Kingdom

For the practicing magician, Quabbalist or yogi, the use of alchemical elixirs as an aid to ritual, meditation, and magical operation will greatly enhance the results. From the astrological point of view, each elixir provides the saturnian groundwork for the plutonian transformation that is required to elevate the consciousness. Each elixir according to its analogy will provide closer contact with the sphere one wishes to experience, as the elixir tunes the physical, astral, and mental bodies to the chosen sphere. In application to healing, this is essential as disharmony must be cleared up on all planes if there is to be a permanent effect.

Following is a brief discussion of each planet and its alchemical significance, and a list of planetary analogies with the plants related to them. This list is by no means complete in any regard. The Alchemist should make their own serious study of Astrology and herbalism in order to understand and intelligently apply what is given in this book.

The Moon

The Moon represents the Water principle, the reflective and transparent properties of materia, and the nature of crystalline formation. It is also rules the subconscious mind and the etheric substrate of matter. This is the octave at which the Alchemist acts most directly in alchemical operations, thus the understanding of the Moon and the etheric tides of matter is a great deal of what mundane Alchemy is all about.

The Moon is the universal solvent at the etheric level, so it is here that the Alchemist begins their work, not only dissolving past tendencies of the subconscious mind (*solve* phase), but also the substance of materia in the laboratory. It is through the bringing together (conjunction) of inner and outer in the laboratory (both the inner and outer laboratory) that the Alchemist begins to see what quantum physics is just learning in its fledgling stages – which is that the observer affects the results. This is why the Moon rules mirrors – the universe has a reflective component (which everything has at some level). To a certain extent, what we see or discover at any level is a reflection of our own selves.

The etheric matrix is most pliable at certain phases of the Moon, thus certain actions are more easily performed at particular points in the lunar cycle. These tides can be replicated by the Alchemist to some degree through the art of physical manipulation, or by the active application of magical knowledge. For instance, when working with the creation of alchemical plant preparations, the *solve* phase (separation into various components) proceeds the best during the waxing of the Moon when the Moon separates and moves to the opposition of the Sun. In the *coagula* phase (when the materials are recombined) the period from Full to New Moon is most auspicious.

The zenith (overhead) position, and the nadir, ascendant and descendant positions of the Moon all have powerful effects on the etheric substrate, which in turn affects matter and psychology. The polarized light of the Moon can make it possible to see into the etheric substrate and thus the phenomenon of apparitions and such are more frequent during this time. The magician-Alchemist uses the lunar cycles to materialize various evoked forces and forms. The Moon is related to the matrix of all form and is *Yesod* in the Quabbala.

Planetary Principles in the Vegetable Kingdom

Lunar Plants in Application

Moon ruled plants affect the subconscious mind. Those involved in hypnosis or auto-hypnosis will find that, when properly impregnated for the desire at hand, these herbs have a powerful effect on the subconscious mind. Any intent, such as a wish to get rid of a certain bad habit, etc., put into a lunar alchemical elixir affects the lunar sphere of our being on all planes.

The lunar herbs can provoke memories of past lives. They provide a channel through the space-time matrix of consciousness, enabling clear perception either through vision or feeling, of past experiences. This can help the Alchemist become aware of the reason for the presence of certain habits which are quite unexplainable from the mundane point of view. If lunar elixirs are impregnated properly in the alchemical manner, karma from the past in the form of bad habits can be lessened in strength or completely eliminated, depending upon the strength and impetus of the causal stress. In many cases the subconscious is the unwitting carrier of our fears and complexes from past lives. A proper regimen with this type of elixir will help to remove such burdensome fears and reactions to the environment which we carry, but which are totally useless, and are only stumbling blocks in our path to the light.

Lunar elixirs are an immense aid in astral projection. The moon at one level has rulership of the astral plane, and lunar elixirs increase awareness of astral form and function. They also produce an interest in common matters and the home environment, and will enhance receptivity and appreciation of the simpler things in life. Use of these elixirs gives grace to the gait and easier attunement to those around you, putting

Herbal Alchemy

you into rhythm with the crowd. The Moon's herbs increase sensitivity and imagination. Their physical therapeutic properties are emetic, alterative, sedative.

Plants of the Moon

Common name	Latin name	Part used
Arrowhead (Wapatoo)	Sagittaria sagittifolia	tubers
Burnet, Lesser	Sanguisorba officinalis	herb, root
Cabbage	Brassica oleracea	leaf
Caltrops (Water Chestnut)	Trapa natans	tuber
Chickweed	Stellaria media	herb
Clary Sage	Salvia sclarea	leaf (fresh & dry)
Cucumber	Cucumis sativus	fruit, seed
Dog's Tooth Violet	Erythronium dens canis	root
Lettuce	Lactuca sativa	leaf
Loosestrife	Lysimacha vulgaris	herb
Lotus Root	Nelumbo nucifera	fresh root
Moonwort (Honesty/Money Plant)	Lunaria annua	leaf
Orach (Mountain Spinach)	Atriplex hortensis	leaf
Orpine	Sedum telephium	leaf, plant
Privet	Ligustrum vulgare	flower, leaf
Purslane	Portulaca oleracea (sativa)	leaf
Roses, White	Rosa (species) i.e. Rosa rugosa alba	petals
Watercress	Nasturtium officinale	leaf, flower, seed
Willow Tree	Salix (species)	bark

Planetary Principles in the Vegetable Kingdom

The Sun

The Sun is the physical representation of the life force for our solar system. Its glyph is the circle-point mandala. The Sun provides us with each planetary principle, thus it contains within it all that is possible within our sphere of experience. All planets in our solar system are variations of the solar force and form – extensions and concrete representations of its energy and cycles of manifestation. The Sun represents the fire element and the electric fluid at the mundane level. For us, the Sun is healing in nature and life giving. At the esoteric level the Sun represents the connection to the center of all centers, the creative force of the universe.

Solar flare activity has a profound effect upon the Earth, and can actually be seen in the display of northern lights – charged particles which ionize the atmosphere. The cycle of solar flares also has powerful influences on the course of civilizations, and everyday matters. Meditation upon the Sun will reveal many mysteries for the Alchemist.

Together the Sun and Moon represent the two great elemental forces operating in our sphere. These are the elements of Fire and Water, the electromagnetic fluid or etheric substrate which makes all form possible. The varieties of the interactions of these two fluids or elements are represented by the different planetary forces. The Sun and Moon are complimentary halves – one could not exist without the other. All alchemical operations take these two forces into account at every juncture. The Sun rules the metal gold and is *Tiphareth* in the Quabbala.

Solar Plants in Application

Sun ruled plants affect the soul in its positive phase of manifestation. The positive phase of manifestation is our idea of ourselves as progressive entities. The solar vibration helps us realize our evolutionary epoch as an individual personality among many other such personalities, and it helps us to synthesize and synchronize our goals with those of the macrocosm. In this sense solar plants are ego fortifiers, but with a universal purpose. As the planets would die and decay without the Sun, so would our world around us fall apart were it not for the strong solar force manifesting from us as ego (cosmic purpose). The Sun represents the myths of Osiris, and of Hercules in his monumental strength.

Solar elixirs are recommended for any sort of inferiority complex. They will bolster and strengthen, and give a sense of purpose beyond the norm. For those with weaker wills, Sun ruled herbs provide a springboard for more positive action. They also bestow the quality of generosity, and can help immensely those unlucky enough to be endowed with a mean or stingy character.

For those more mystically inclined, solar plants when properly impregnated will lead to the understanding of the purpose of our solar system, and will create awareness of the higher will in manifestation. They give great ambition, courage, and self reliance; and bestow dignity, authority, and the ability to manage and regulate. As representatives of the vitality principle in our cosmos, solar herbs can remedy apathy or pull one out of an unproductive period. The Sun represents the divine creative force in our solar system, and its elixirs enhance the creative principle within us. Their physical therapeutic properties are usually sudorific and cardiac.

Planetary Principles in the Vegetable Kingdom

Plants of the Sun

Common name	Latin name	Part used
Almond	Amygdalus communis	nut
Angelica	Angelica archangelica	root, leaf, seed
Bay Tree	Lauris noblis	leaf
Burnet, Great	Sanguisorba officinalis	herb, root
Calendula	Calendula officinalis	flower, leaf
Celandine	Chelidonium majus	herb
Centaury	Centaurium erythaea	herb, leaf
Chamomile	Matricaria recutita	flower
Dandelion	Taraxacum officinale	leaf, flower, root
Eyebright	Euphrasia officinalis	herb
Heliotrope	Heliotrope arborescens	flower
Jerusalem Artichoke	Helianthus tuberosus	tuber, flower
Lily of the Valley	Convallaria magalis	herb, flower, leaf
Lovage	Levisticum officinale	leaf, stalks
Marigold	Tagetes (species)	flower
Rue, Garden	Ruta graveolens	herb
St. Johnswort	Hypericum perforatum	herb
Sunflower	Helianthus annuus	seed, flower
Viper's Bugloss	Echium vulgare	herb

Mercury

The planet Mercury represents Akasha (ether) which contains all possibilities or pathways. The astrological symbol for Mercury is composed of the lunar crescent, the circle-point mandala (which represents the Sun), and the equal armed cross, which represents the Earth. These three components form a triad which is of major significance for life and evolution on this planet. The phrase, "Thrice great Toth" (Hermes) relates to this triad. True knowledge, from the alchemical point of view, is derived from both logic (Sun/left brain), and intuition (Moon/right brain). It is the coming together of these two phases or elements of Fire and Water that creates balance (the Akasha Principle) which synthesizes our experiences.

Mercury as the great synthesizer creates pathways or networks between different points in space. As a result of this connection (mercurian process), each point affects the others, so the mercurian process makes possible the reciprocal contact of the venusian process.

Mercury measures all things, whether time, weight, distance or height, and is the planet of geometry. Because of their measurable qualities, all materials respond to particular cosmic frequencies. In many cultures there are specific shapes and proportions which have occult significance and are known to have particular effects. If this sounds like superstition, consider the simple art of antenna making. To pick up a broadcast from a certain station, the transmitter antenna and the receiver antenna must have a certain corresponding length ratio. The length of the wire is the key to picking up any particular frequencies. Every object and shape in the universe has a particularly frequency that it responds to. For instance, every planet emits a different radio frequency that can be picked up on our earth with an antenna tuned for that frequency.

The science of communication is Mercury's province. However, from the Alchemist's point of view, communication has a deeper meaning. It refers to the ability to perceive anything by any senses whatsoever, and to understanding that what is perceived has a revelatory nature. Any thing can inform you of its essential self by intuition as well as by observation as we normally think of it.

Because Mercury has within its realm the principles of cosmic intuition and knowing, it is called the messenger of

Planetary Principles in the Vegetable Kingdom

the gods. To relate to the inner nature of the cosmos in order to understand the outer is represented by the Caduceus of Hermes-Mercury-Toth. This is the symbol of the cerebral-spinal system, and within this structure is the "royal road," or the path of the Alchemist. Mercury's knowledge is that vibratory rate is the key to the nature of all things. For instance, it tells us that light and matter are the same thing but at different frequency.

Meditation on the planet Mercury leads the Alchemist to the doorway of an inexhaustible supply of knowledge. It is the symbol of the Magician. The metal for the planet Mercury is quicksilver, and it is *Hod* in the Quabbala.

Plants of Mercury in Application

Mercury ruled plants affect the thinking and reasoning process. They give a keen, versatile mind, wit and mental resourcefulness. Those who feel debilitated because of a sluggish mind will find that these elixirs quicken all perceptions to a great degree. Mercurian herbs also give the ability to associate one set of phenomena with another more easily. For writers, orators, etc., mercurian elixirs will provide an ease of comprehension that will speed up their work.

The herbs of Mercury are important from an occult standpoint because when mixed with solar and lunar herbs, they harmonize the total being, allowing easier access to the akashic essence. Magically they are connected with mythological figures Hermes and Toth. The elixirs affect the Mercury chakra (sephira), which is related to the power of the word. They dynamize thought and words with the Akasha Principle, which is the substratum of all things; thus, they enable the use of the great power of the word and the ability to see truth. Mixed with Moon herbs, they give psychic receptivity. Mixed with Sun herbs, they give telepathic sending abilities to a marked degree.

By taking a Mercury elixir as a regular regimen, the Magician can open up to the sphere of Magic on the mental plane. This will allow progress in this art at a much faster pace than otherwise. If an occultist has a problem contacting any sphere they are working with, a Mercury elixir will create a link from the microcosm to the macrocosmic principle of the desired sphere. This can be a valuable aid to mediums and magicians who practice the art of evocation. Their physical and therapeutic properties are nervine, alterative and mental.

Plants of Mercury

Common name	Latin name	Part used
Bracken Fern	Pteris aquiline	leaf, new shoots
Calamint	Calamintha grandiflora	herb
Caraway	Carum carvi	seed, herb
Carrots	Daucus carota sativus	root, herb
Celery	Apium graveleons	herb, seed, root
Dill	Anethum graveolens	seed, herb
Elecampane	Inula helenium	root
Fennel	Foeniculum vulgare	seed, herb
Fenugreek	Trigonella foenum-graecum	seed, herb
Good King Henry	Chenopodium bonus-henricus	herb
Hazelnut	Corylus (species)	nut, twig
Horehound	Marribium vulgare	herb
Licorice	Glycyrrhiza glabra (and species)	root
Maidenhair Fern	Adiantum (species)	fresh herb
Majoram & Oregano	Origanum (species)	herb
Mullberry Tree	Morus Nigra (and species)	fruit
Parsley	Petroselinum crispum	herb, root

Planetary Principles in the Vegetable Kingdom

Plants of Mercury (*continued*)

Common name	Latin name	Part used
Queen Anne's Lace	Daucus carota	root, herb
Rosemary	Rosmarinus officinalis	leaf, flower
Southernwood	Artemisia camphorate	leaf, herb
Valerian	Valeriana officinalis	root

Venus

Venus is harmony and balance within our solar system – grace and ease of movement at all levels, from the perpetual motion of infinitely divisible particles to the movement of people upon a dance floor. The Sufis through their meditative dance understand this connection very well. Venus operates on all levels via the magnetic attraction of one body to another which allows aggregates to form. It allows discrete components to come together, for instance, so that a body of knowledge can be shared (the Jupiter process).

Venus is the social lubricant that creates and sustains civilization. It is the principle of coming together (communion) with other people, which makes life easier and more harmonious. For this particular evolutionary epoch Venus is the goal that humanity strives to understand and implement.

In order for any element or being to sustain a relationship to another element or being, the venusian principle has to be in place. It is the cosmic dance, and in reality this interaction or dance is what most scientists study. They observe the interactions of materia, which is essentially observing the etiquette, if you will, of substance – but they do not observe the reason for the etiquette.

Alchemical science goes beyond this outer form. For instance, a scientist can talk about the attraction or repulsion of one molecule for another, or another human being for another, or they can talk about sexuality in terms of what they observe — but what no scientist can tell you is why. There are Alchemical answers for the why question. Why do chemicals do this or why do people do that? What is the deeper meaning? The Alchemist understands that there are threads which connect the inner with the outer. These connections are the true nature of Venus and are shown to us via analogy of form and interaction.

The Alchemist knows that form speaks to us intuitively, by its very nature, and explains itself in its relationship to all other form. This is the concept of relativity, but at the right brain level. From a venusian point of view, relationships, whether atomic, molecular or human bonds, exist to bring awareness to a new level via reciprocity, which in turn creates a new state of being.

Venus rules the plant kingdom. All plants, whatever their particular attributes have a general venusian overtone. Feng Shui is a venusian art form and science that attempts to create harmonious energies in our environment through the judicious placement of certain forms. The metal of Venus is copper, and in the Quabbala it is Netzach.

Plants of Venus in Application

Plants ruled by Venus affect celestial form and magnetic qualities. They give the ability to attract, aesthetic appreciation and refinement of the senses. Artists, actors and designers will find these elixirs helpful in their work. Venusian herbs also enhance the taste perceptions, promote affection,

Planetary Principles in the Vegetable Kingdom

give an amiable disposition, and make one more psychically sensitive to astral influences.

Herbs of Venus are very good for inducing a quality of lightness in the personality. Social directors, restauranteurs, and those who deal in amusement will find that these elixirs provide the consciousness necessary for promoting and producing their events and establishments. Fashion designers and interior decorators will find that direct contact with the Venus sphere will bring on such a spate of ideas that they could not handle them all in one lifetime. For those who feel that they lack charm, or some of the softer human qualities, the Venus elixir will help induce the right vibration in the aura to amend that deficiency. Venusian elixirs also make one much more attractive. Most people find this hard to believe, because they do not realize that attraction has to do mainly with invisible vibration, rather than with outward appearance.

Venus elixirs promote harmony and balance within our selves and in our dealings with others. Through their effects on the Venus chakra, venusian alchemical elixirs will give access to the realm of the astral that is intimately connected with the workings and forces of the magic of nature. For those who make herbal Alchemy their life work, elixirs of Venus will open the sphere of consciousness to the secrets of the plant kingdom. Nature cultists will find the elixirs most illuminating as they will give conscious contact with the various deities of long past nature religions. Their physical therapeutic properties are demulcent, anti nephritic and emetic.

Herbal Alchemy

Plants of Venus

Common name	Latin name	Part used
Alfalfa	Medicago sativa	herb
Alkanet	Anchusa officinalis	root
Apples	Prunus malus	fruit
Bishop's Weed	Ammi majus	herb
Brambles (Raspberry, Blackberry, etc.)	Rubus (species)	leaf, fruit
Bugle	Ajuga reptens	herb
Carnations/Pinks	Dianthus (species)	flower
Catnip	Nepeta cataria	herb
Cherry Tree	Prunus (species)	bark, fruit
Cinnamon	Cinnamomum zeylanicum	bark
Coltsfoot	Tussilago farfara	leaf, flower
Daisy, English	Bellis perennis	leaf, root
Daisy	Chrysanthemum leucanthemum	herb, flower
Feverfew	Tanacetum parthenium	leaf
Goldenrod	Solidago (species)	leaf
Gooseberry	Ribes grossularia	fruit, leaf
Ground Ivy (Gill-Over-the Ground)	Glechoma hederaceae	leaf, flower
Heal-All	Prunella vulgaris	herb
Lady's Mantle	Alchemilla vulgaris	herb, root
Marshmallow	Althea officinalis	leaf, root, flower
Pears	Pyrus communis	fruit
Peas	Pisum sativum	seed
Peppermint	Mentha piperata	herb
Primrose	Primula veris	leaf, flower
Red Clover	Trifolium pratens	leaf, flower
Rocket, Sweet	Hesperis matronalis	flower, leaf
Roses	Rosa (species)	flower, fruit
Sorrel, Wood	Oxalis acetosa	leaf, herb
Sorrel, Garden	Rumex acetosa	leaf, herb
Sorrel, Sheep	Rumex acetosella	leaf, herb

Planetary Principles in the Vegetable Kingdom

Plants of Venus (*continued*)

Common name	Latin name	Part used
Spearmint	Mentha spicata	herb
Strawberry	Fragaria rosaceae	leaf, fruit
Strawberry Blite (Beetberry)	Amaranthus blitus	fruit
Sweet Cicely	Osmoriza claytonis	herb
Woodruff, Sweet	Gallium odoratum	leaf, flower

Mars

Mars is the Akasha Principle in action, the movement through time and space which Mercury measures. Mars is essentially the motion that we see as the active universe, or life. Form is created by movement, and all form moves as matter goes through cycles of being. The nature of form is to interact with other forms. There is no movement in this universe that does not act upon all other things. This is the nature of Mars.

The symbol of Mars is the pentagram, or five pointed star. Each point represents one of the five elements. The power of the five elements reside in this pentagrammaton. It is the symbol of the active Alchemist and the flow of all energies. It represents fire, heat, energy and activation which is the catalyst for all reactions.

Every aspect of life is the movement of materia from one point to another. Indeed, our very thoughts are movements through time and space. We are who we are by the psychological and physical movements of our being. Each of us is as distinct as a fingerprint in our own unique way of moving.

The active formation of organic metallic compounds and the process of oxidation (which is important in alchemical work) is ruled by the planet Mars. Whether it is the production and action of electrolytes in our cells or the process of combining the salts of various plants with their sulphurs, it is Mars at work. Observation of any form in its active phase reveals the personality or signature of the form to the Alchemist. The metal of Mars is iron, and it is *Geburah* in the Quabbala.

Plants of Mars in Application

Mars ruled herbs affect the physical counterpart of the soul, and create awareness of oneself as an organism. The history of the fight for survival is one of the many mystical experiences of the Mars sephira. Use of the martian elixir will reveal the true universal purpose behind the instinct for self preservation.

Mars herbs are wonderful tonics when mixed with solar herbs. The elixirs give great energy and will benefit anyone who lacks such energy. Those who work in occupations requiring a great deal of strength will find these most suitable. The elixirs also give self reliance and independence of attitude, and make a person more spontaneous.

Mars stimulates the passions and tones the muscles. Those who are meek by nature may find that the martian elixirs make them more gregarious, and physically more passionate and attractive. In general they help to release the action potential of your soul. Since Mars is the Akasha Principle in action, when martian elixirs are mixed with any of the other planetary herbs, they stimulate the other herbs to a greater state of activity.

The mystical experience that comes about through the use of martian elixirs is the knowledge of space-time as the pentagrammaton in action. Thus, on the physical plane, through the activated essence of the martian elixir, one

Planetary Principles in the Vegetable Kingdom

can bring about all types of magical phenomenon related to telekinesis (movement of objects by thought). For those involved in the magic of evocation, a mixture of a Mars, Moon, and Mercury elixirs will help produce the physical vehicle for manifestation on the Earth plane. Their physical therapeutic properties are stimulative, caustic and tonic.

Plants of Mars

Common name	Latin name	Part used
Aloes	Aloe vera	sap from the leaf
Barberry	Berberis vulgaris	bark, root bark, fruit
Black Pepper	Piper nigrum	dried unripe fruit
Chives	Allium schoenoprasum	herb
Coriander	Coriandrum sativum	herb, seed
Cranesbill	Geranium sanguineum (and species)	root, leaf
Cumin	Cuminum cyminum	seed
Garlic	Allium sativa	herb
Gentian	Gentiana (species)	root
Hawthorne	Crataegus oxycantha	fruit
Horseradish	Cochlearia armoralia	root, leaf
Leeks	Allium porrum	leaf, bulb
Madder	Rubia tinctorum	root
Masterwort	Imperatora ostruthium	root
Mugwort	Artemisia vulgaris	leaf
Mustard	Brassica alba & nigra	herb, seed
Nettles	Urtica dioica, urens	herb
Onions	Allium cepa	bulb, leaf
Pepper, Hot	Capsicum annuum (and species)	fruit
Pine	Pinus sylvestris	bark, needles
Radish	Raphanus sativus	root, seed pods
Rhubarb	Rheum rhaponticum	leaf stalks (leaf is not edible)
Wormwood	Artemesia absinthium	leaf

Jupiter

Jupiter is the expansive principle in our solar system. In the Vedic pantheon, it is represented by Vishnu, the preserver. Jupiter's role is to preserve and codify truth, as it is commonly perceived, via laws. Jupiter is a speculator and connected with the formation of religions and bodies of legal knowledge ("speculative" because both law and religion are simply guesses at divine purpose). It is the planet of the theories and opinions which are part of the cosmic process, and it is ever seeking toward expansion of understanding.

In its larger sense, Jupiter rules institutions that evaluate observations and the meaning or validity of results. It is the energy which allows us to compare discoveries, share knowledge, and build upon the work and knowledge of others. This principle of sharing and comparing is at work even on the subatomic level – from the cosmic point of view, the Jupiter principle is latent within every particle of matter.

Through the study of (and meditation upon) Jupiter, the Alchemist realizes that human law, religion and other formalized ritual functions are actually a product of the movement of subatomic forces, and thus elemental in nature. Every human endeavor is a constantly changing speculative model, based upon the very generalized formation of a group of forces and forms in a space-time context. Jupiter also rules humor and laughter, so it should be apparent from this that we should not take our speculations – law, religion and other institutions – too seriously less we become bloated, unwieldy and overbearing in our presence.

Jupiter preserves, but only so that a coherent body of information can be available to advance knowledge in the light of evolutionary change. The Jupiter aggregate functions in organisms in genetic code (a collection of information), and in the intelligence that draws upon past experience to develop alternative strategies in order to adapt to a changing environment. Without this function, life as we know it would not exist at all.

So Jupiter represents the accumulation of a body of experiences that are utilized by any being to develop itself in accord with cosmic purpose. Another element of this process is optimism (which is also of the nature of Jupiter) which surely must be active for any being to compile its knowledge of experience for a forward-looking evolutionary journey. The term optimism is obviously related to optimal, or optimal operating and optimization, so, one can readily see how the process of evolutionary change (optimization) and optimism are connected.

From the point of view of the herbal Alchemist, plant classification according to their natures and uses is the province of the jupiterian function. Jupiter rules the metal tin, and is *Chesed* in the Quabbala.

Plants of Jupiter in Application

Jupiter ruled plants are benefic in application. They help to preserve the body and promote healthy growth, and are the natural healing herbs of this planetary system. Their effect on the mind is to promote affinity for, and understanding of ritual form from a cosmic point of view. From an exoteric point of view, this is law and religion, so these elixirs are of particular interest to religious leaders, doctors, lawyers, etc. Jupiter elixirs give a ceremonial tact and because of the induced vibration can put the Alchemist into situations of pomp and circumstance. They also bring in a wealth vibration and open up psychic channels for growth and expansion, materially as well as spiritually.

Herbal Alchemy

Charged in the alchemical manner, Jupiter elixirs enable the magician to penetrate into the sphere of legality for our macrocosm, increasing awareness of the principles of the tetragrammaton. Jupiter is the great benefactor of our solar system, and thus represents the principle of what is often called divine grace. If mixed with a solar herbal elixir it will give the Alchemist access to the highest planes of form where they will see what role mercy and kindness have to play in our evolutionary process. Elixirs of Jupiter will create opportunities to give with joy and grace.

For the philosophically inclined, Jupiter-Mercury combinations will give a profound insight into any system of philosophy and its part in the cosmic scheme. This combination will also put the Alchemist in touch via intuition with the great avatars and their teachings, in order to learn and to teach others. A Jupiter-Mercury elixir produces a light heartedness and mirthfulness which can be very useful to those with a predisposition to depression or gloominess.

The physical therapeutic properties of Jupiter ruled plants are anabolic and anti-spasmodic.

Plants of Jupiter

Common name	Latin name	Part used
Agrimony	Agrimonia eupatoria	herb
Artichoke, Globe	Cynaria scolymus	leaf stalk
Asparagus	Asparagus officinalis	new shoots
Basswood/ Linden Tree	Tillia (species)	leaf, flower
Borage	Borago officinalis	leaf, flower
Chervil	Anthriscus cereifolium	leaf
Chestnut, Sweet	Castanea sativa	nut, leaf
Chick Peas	Cicer arietinum	seed
Costmary	Chrysanthemum balsamita	fresh leaf
Eggplant	Solanum melongena	fruit

Planetary Principles in the Vegetable Kingdom

Plants of Jupiter (continued)

Common name	Latin name	Part used
Grapes	Vitus vinifera	fruit, leaf
Houseleek	Sempervivum tectorum	fresh leaf
Hyssop	Hyssopus officinalis	herb
Lady's Thistle/ Milk Thistle	Silybum marianum	herb, root, seed, hull
Lemon Balm	Melissa officinalis	herb
Liverwort	Hepatica acutiloba	leaf, flower
Lungwort	Pulmonaria officinalis	leaf, flower
Maple Tree	Acer saccharinum (and species)	sap, syrup
Oak Tree	Quercus (species)	bark, fruit
Olive	Olea Europaea	fruit, leaf, bark
Plum	Prunus domestica	fruit
Sage	Salvia officinalis	leaf
Squash & Pumpkins	Curcubita (species)	fruit, flower
Walnut	Juglans (species)	nut
Witch Grass (Twitch Grass, Dog's Grass)	Agropyrum repens	root

Saturn

Saturn represents matter in its densest manifestation, in other words it is the densest manifestation of the Akasha Principle (ether). It rules the metal lead. All of the manifest cosmos, no matter what dimension of time and space, has a saturnian element to some degree. To exist in space and be recognized as form, a form must have limits and a foundation. Atoms, flowers, buildings, and people all have specific forms. Saturn is the nature of form, it is the superstructure in which everything takes its space-time relevance and relatedness. It represents congealed electromagnetic and atomic forces, the etheric substrate or lines of force, essentially all frameworks. It also is the laws of the natural world.

Herbal Alchemy

The most basic characteristics of form – weight, substance, height, depth, width, etc. – are saturnian. However, these properties should not be confused with their measurement, which is a function of Mercury. Saturn is the necessary congealing factor which creates those properties. It is the principle of form which allows form to happen.

Time also is ruled by Saturn, hence the saturnian old man figure "Father Time." (Once again, remember that the measurement of time is a mercurian function.) Time is measured by the movement and relative position of form, whether it is the rotation of the Earth in relation to the Sun and Moon, or the vibration of cesium atoms in an atomic clock. Time must have space in order to manifest, and vice versa.

All other planetary principles on the planes of manifestation must have a saturnian foundation to be recognizable by our five senses. Saturn is represented by the number three, which relates to the three elements Fire, Water and Air which interact to create the element Earth.

All things manifest in the universe have a relational value, and relationships of any kind are only possible because of Saturn's limitations. For a form to exist, there must also be the rest of the universe which is not that particular form. Saturn is the boundaries that define a form as distinct from the rest of manifestation. Yet, by defining a particular form, all other forms are also defined. No one thing is of and by itself, but is a part of the whole. No one single object in the universe could manifest without every other object being in its appropriate place. Everything that exists is totally dependent on everything else that exists.

This principle gets us deep into the very esoteric nature of Saturn. Form truly is a cyclic manifestation. It is not permanent or static as our senses would like us to believe.

Planetary Principles in the Vegetable Kingdom

Nothing is really solid. Everything constantly vibrates and moves. The Alchemist would say that every object is really an attitude, meaning that it wishes to be observed as such and such at some period in time and space. Thus psychology and matter are considered to be one and the same – a curious perspective for most to understand.

The contemplation of Saturn reveals the nature of cycles and the origins of matter as we perceive it. It reveals to us that the four elements are essentially points of perspective that exist on the edges of the circle-point mandala. That is why the Alchemist meditates on the center-point within the circle, as it is from this perspective only that the whole can be viewed and understood as one.

Saturn contains many mysteries such as the essential nature of the laws of cause and effect, karma and evolution. The term Satan is a derivative from Saturn. Mythologically in some circles, Satan is considered to be the great deceiver – because form is not what it seems to be. This is not to take up any theological implications for any particular religious group, but it does show that there was some glimmer of understanding about the scientific nature of form even if the theology and understanding was limited in some groups. In this light it is interesting to note that the term Satan means "he who comes down" – meaning literally, to manifest. It is also interesting that Lucifer – another term for Satan – means "light bearer."

This implies that it is within the process of manifestation, and in the geometry of the universe itself wherein enlightenment resides. Matter thus redeems itself through its own light. Esoterically "redemption" means knowledge and wisdom (being "saved" from ignorance, if you will). It is not the "redemption" of the theologies of various religious institutions. Separating the bad theology from first principles we can begin to understand the nature of the universe. There are many mysteries tied up in Saturn that relate to the science of Alchemy. Saturn is *Binah* in the Quabbala.

Plants of Saturn in Application

Saturn ruled plants enhance the structures of life. They give a sobriety of disposition, and increase awareness of karmic limitations. The Saturn elixir gives steadiness, solidity of purpose, subtlety, diplomacy, patience, and an ability to work better on the physical plane. It brings the Alchemist into the realm of the Saturn chakra and the laws of cause and effect and their relationship to karma, and laws of physics, and so forth.

For those who have difficulty finishing projects that they start, saturnian elixirs will have an earthing effect which can bring things to completion. The same holds true for those with many ideas but no opportunity to realize them.

A saturnian elixir mixed with a mercurian one will bring in knowledge contained in secret magical manuscripts hidden away in private libraries that the student of Alchemy would not normally have access to. This is because the Mercury-Saturn vibration contains all hidden knowledge of a magical nature. This combination will also give a profound insight into the oldest magical traditions which once existed and are now defunct.

Magicians with a strong interest in producing physical effects will find in the elixirs of Saturn the essential vibratory rate needed to produce a variety of physical plane materializations. Generally speaking, any other elixir mixed with a Saturn elixir will be earthed, which makes saturnian elixirs of great value for working on heavy physical plane phenomena.

Planetary Principles in the Vegetable Kingdom

Their physical therapeutic properties are refrigerant, antipyretic, sedative, styptic and astringent.

Plants of Saturn

Common name	Latin name	Part used
Amaranth	Amaranthus hypochondriacus	plant, seed
Ash Tree	Fraxinus excelsior and Americana	leaf tips, bark
Barley	Hordeum distichon (and species)	seed
Beech Tree	Fagus sylvatica	leaf, seed
Chicory (endive, escarole, witloof, etc.)	Cicorium endiva, intybus, etc.	root, leaf
Corn Flower	Centaurea cyanus	flower
Crosswort	Galium cruciata	herb, leaf
Elm Tree	Ulmus campestris	bark
Hartstongue Fern	Scolopendium vulgare	fronds
Hawkweed	Hieracium pilosella	herb
Horsetail	Equisetum (species)	plant
Knotgrass	Polyganum aviculare	herb
Mountain Ash	Pyrus Americana	bark, fruit
Mullein	Verbascum thapsis	leaf, root, flower
Parsnip	Pastinaca sativus	root, leaf, seed
Plantain	Plantago (species)	leaf, seed
Poplar Tree/ Aspen	Populus tremuloides	bark
Potato	Solanum tuberosum	tuber
Royal Fern, Ostrich Fern	Osmunda (species)	root, new fronds
Rye	Secale cereale	seed
Shepherd's Purse	Capsella bursa-pastoris	plant
Spinach	Spinacia oleracea	leaf
Tamarind	Tamarindus indica	leaf, fruit
Wheat	Triticum aestivum	seed
Yarrow	Achillea millefolium	herb, flower

Uranus

Uranus is the planet of life force – chi energy – the creative energy of the universe, enlivening all matter and the source of all movement. It is the electricity and oxygen in the very atmosphere we breath. As the only principle that can disrupt and rearrange the form of matter in an instant, it is also the planet of magic. It rules the science of Astrology and the principle of enlightenment, and is the universal spark from which all electromagnetic polarity flows. Uranus represents absolute freedom from the bondage of illusion and gives mastery of all that exists. It is pure energy that knows no bounds.

Uranus is represented by the number one and is Kether on the Tree of Life in the Quabbala system. Uranus represents the connection of our solar system with other life forms in other planetary systems, and in particular is connected with the star Sirius, which was of great importance to the ancient Egyptians. It is the most physical representation of the Akasha Principle on this plane.

It is what science calls intelligence, and in this aspect its process can be characterized by the feedback loop – act, observe and analyze the results of the action, and change the next action accordingly. Thus, Uranus rules science, and is the principle of evolution (and revolution). It destroys old forms. All life forms try to move through life unhampered, always attempting to impose their needs on their environment. When the way they do this creates resistance to their imposition, then the organism must change its behavior, change its needs, or face extinction.

In a mundane sense, all of our neural networks are designed around the uranian operation of flowing energy, and the feedback loop. Uranus rules the metals aluminum and zinc.

Planetary Principles in the Vegetable Kingdom

Plants of Uranus in Application

Uranus ruled plants affect the electromagnetic (*chi*) energy in our mental, astral and physical bodies. These plants impart an extraordinary energy and kinetic quality to the aura which influences the structure of surrounding matter. Psychokinetic abilities are greatly enhanced by these elixirs. Practitioners of any type of alternative therapy such as acupuncture, electrotherapy, etc. will find they provide insight and intuition into unconventional modes of healing.

Uranian herbs provide the instant insight and intuition which is called *satori* in Zen practice. Those who follow the path of magic will find that Uranus ruled plants create the vibration necessary to develop and bring various energies through to the physical plane. For inventors, scientists, or researchers, uranian elixirs will reveal a wealth of ideas and concepts that can further their endeavors. These elixirs produce intense intellectual activity and quicken the mind. For those seeking to discover their own particular genius, the elixirs will bring to the fore-front one's own natural talents.

Generally, the uranian herbs create greater electrical activity in the brain and throughout the body, and so have an energizing effect. They are very good for those who feel depleted and need to be recharged. The electrical activity created by these herbs can also help in weight reduction, toning the physical body, and to keep one youthful looking. Uranian elixirs will also keep the Alchemist in tune with the newest ideas and concepts, and produce a forward looking vibration in the aura. This makes them very good for understanding and relating to younger generations, and for avoiding becoming stagnant in thought and outlook. Whatever is considered new and revolutionary resonates with the Uranus vibration. Computers and computer science are Uranus ruled, and anyone involved in these will be greatly benefitted by the use of uranian elixirs. Uranus also enhances the will and gives a strong form to life energies, which in turn gives the ability to cut through the static and negative dispositions of others. They also enhance the intuitive capacity to see into the future and will help to guide courses of action based on these insights. Uranian elixirs are a great help in astral projection and telepathic exercises.

Plants of Uranus

Common name	Latin name	Part used
Chia	Salvia Hispanica	seed
Ginger	Zingiber officinalis	root
Gingko Biloba	Gingko biloba	leaf, nut
Ginseng	Panax cinquefolius, Panax ginseng	root
Gotu Kola	Centella Asiatica	leaf
Kava Kava	Piper methysticum	root
Pineapple	Ananas comosus	fruit
Scullcap	Scuttelaria latifolia	herb
Sea Holly	Eryngium campestre	root
Sensitive Plant	Mimosa pudica	leaf
Siberian Ginseng	Eleutherococcus senticosus	root, leaf
Wild Ginger	Asarum Canadanse, Europ	root
Yerba Mate	Ilex paraguensis	leaf

Neptune

Neptune represents the universal solvent – that which dissolves form. It is no coincidence that Neptune rules meditation. For the Alchemist to be able to see beyond the restrictions of their limited personalities and insights, meditation is necessary. It breaks the bonds and limitations imposed

Planetary Principles in the Vegetable Kingdom

by form in the space-time continuum. Neptune is the waters that refresh, and the true meaning of baptism is part of the mysteries of Neptune.

Neptune is amorphous and shows no boundaries – it goes beyond the individual and reveals the meaning of the universal ferment. It refreshes, and dissolves the chains of ignorance that keep one shackled to the conventional. It is the sea of life and all its manifestations viewed from a larger perspective. It is the myriad of possibilities or potential of the Akasha Principle, the non-formed.

Beyond each individual ego are many other such egos, life forms and materia with their own different agendas. Neptune represents all that is usually considered the non-self. In Neptune the Alchemist can rise above the individual ego and perceive themselves as a small part of the whole. Without this big picture there is really no knowing that is not subject to the limits of time and space.

To capture the essence of the Philosophers Stone the great process of *solve* (dissolution) must first run its course. Then with the understanding, gained from wider perspective of Neptune, the next step *coagula* (coalescence) can be performed. A new entity is born from such understanding. In fact, Alchemy is called *spagyra* or *spagyrica* which means near and far, and to take apart and put back together. One must disengage from the self in order to discover the self and its connection with the universal soul.

Neptune is magnetic and healing. Its nature is of the element of Water. The operations of Neptune are needed in all alchemical processes for the work upon Saturn (matter). Neptune working upon Saturn creates energy or life force. The vast oceans on our planet are filled with powerful electrolyte solution, dissolved matter (salts) which with water produces electricity (Uranus), and is the motive fuel of all organisms. Life on Earth has evolved from the sea.

Physical water is one of the most magical substances on Earth. There are many secrets hidden within its nature. All liquids are ruled by Neptune, and the knowledge and understanding of fluidity and its meaning is of great importance to the Alchemist. Symbolically, the action of meditation (Neptune) upon matter (Saturn) produces the same results at one level as the action of physical water upon matter.

Neptune's number is two, as it represents first polarity. It is what allows Saturn to concretize into forms. There is a great mystery in Neptune in that it holds the secret of recognizing all other forms through the study and awareness of one form. A form can only exist in context, thus every form holds the key to all other forms. This is why a shaman in Siberia can throw the bones and see the future, and why tarot cards work. It is the nature of the universe to reveal itself at every moment and instant. Thus, you will read repeatedly in the literature of Alchemy that the secret sought by the Alchemists is everywhere. The golden key is so common as to be unrecognizable.

Neptune rules the metals of potassium and sodium, and in the Quabbala system is *Chokma*.

Plants of Neptune in Application

Neptune ruled plants affect cosmic perceptions, musical and artistic abilities, and general harmony with the flow of natural forces. The neptunian elixirs greatly enhance the ability to perceive the music of the spheres and the flow of cosmic process. They produce sensitivity to external surroundings – perception of the intricacies and delicate

Planetary Principles in the Vegetable Kingdom

details of the fabric of the universe, and its connection with every day life. They have the general effect of refining the senses and creating an aesthetic appreciation for the fine art that manifests in all objects and circumstances. Musicians, painters, dancers, actors, or others involved in any form of artful expression, will find that these elixirs give a heightened creative ability, and access to a vast storehouse of ideas as yet undreamed of. They give artists the capability to transform any perception, whether mental, astral or physical, into any media they work with.

The subtle interconnection of seemingly diverse processes are revealed by Neptune, and thus a powerful intuitive capability is produced. Insight, inspiration, intuition, and psychic receptivity are all enhanced with neptunian elixirs. They create vivid dream states and enhance the Alchemist's capability to astral project as the neptunian vibration loosens the bonds of consciousness with the physical body.

Neptune rules the seas and oceans, and calls us to experience what is beyond our own shores, and to share in the delight of tales of far distant lands, with exotic customs and unusual ways. The elixirs of Neptune aid the ability to understand other points of view, as the ego barriers that surround the individual dissolve so that a true dialogue can occur. They bring us out of ourselves and into a larger world, thus producing contacts with more interesting people. They give a sense of common purpose and reveal to us our place within the cosmic ocean of vibrations.

Treasure hunters, explorers and researchers into obscure matters will find that these elixirs tune them into and guide them to that which they seek via subtle psychic processes.

Neptunian elixirs also impart a mysterious magnetic attractive quality to the aura, which has a strong influence on others and the surrounding environment.

The art of meditation is ruled by Neptune, thus Neptune's elixirs produce profound insights, as they enhance meditation and promote harmony with the cosmic tides. Those who are troubled with erratic sleep will find that neptunian elixirs produce a hypnotic rhythm that can induce relaxation and sleep. For those who feel out of step with things in general, the elixirs will help to synchronize with the environment and people around them.

Neptune also rules the natural rhythms and cycles of the earth and produces a great sense of rhythm for dance – cosmic and otherwise. The elixirs are of great help to anyone in the healing and helping professions as they help to tune in on the problem at hand and to discern solutions to hidden and obscure causes of problems. An elixir of Neptune will promote the understanding of natural healing rhythms, the frequencies of various substances and the electromagnetic field of the aura.

Plants of Neptune

Common name	Latin name	Part used
Agar Agar	Gelidium amonsi	plant
Common Club Moss	Lycopodium claratum	spores
Dulse	Rhodymenia palmata	plant
Flax	Linum usitatissimum	seed
Gum Arabic	Acacia senegal	resin from sap
Irish Moss	Chondrus crispus	plant
Kelp	Laminaria digitata	plant
Slippery Elm	Ulmus rubra	inner bark
Spirulina	various blue/green algae	algae

Planetary Principles in the Vegetable Kingdom

Pluto

Pluto rules transmutation, transformation and regeneration. It is the process of renewal, of new pathways, and the planet which rules the process of Alchemy. In Pluto's realm is the awareness that all materia can be transformed literally into any other type of materia – and that non-material things can be made material and vice versa. Pluto gives knowledge of the different dimensions of time and space, and of the transmutation of energy from one dimension into another. All hidden forces (those not readily discernible) are the province of Pluto.

Quantum physics, and the processes of materialization and dematerialization are plutonian in nature. Although it may seem science fiction, quantum teleportation is already a scientifically proven fact. Experiments and studies at the University of Innsbruck in the 1990s indicate that it is possible to transfer the properties of one photon, electron or atom to another space-time location even if the two are galaxies apart, without them actually traveling through space. Thus the secrets of the Akasha Principle and the axiom, *What is here is there, what is not here is not there,* is slowly beginning to be understood by scientists. Pluto rules the metal platinum.

As the planet of Alchemy, Pluto essentially rules the process of transmutation that is inherent in each plant material and its effect upon us. Thus Pluto ruled plants are each and every plant with which the Alchemist works.

Collection and Preparation of Plants

The ideal way to procure plant material for these purposes is to grow the plants yourself, if at all possible. Just a small garden space, or even a few pots on a window sill, are sufficient to grow much of the plant material needed for alchemical work. It is beyond the scope of this book to provide detailed growing information – that is widely available to the reader elsewhere.

Each Alchemist develops their own working repertoire of plants, based on their own interests, needs and the specifics of their resources. If you have a garden, indoors or outdoors, note carefully which plants adapt well to your conditions and preferred growing techniques, and as much as possible, favor the use of those plants in your alchemical work.

In the preparation of herbal elixirs it is very important not to use any plants treated with chemical pesticides. If you grow your plants, use organic gardening methods; if you buy your plants, always try to get those that are certified organic.

For the gardening Alchemist, there is a comprehensive selection of seeds and plants available from Richters, Goodwood, Ontario. Richters also sells dried herbs. Another excellent resource for seed is J. L. Hudson, Seedsman, La Honda, California. Dried herbs and other items can be purchased from the Frontier Natural Products Co-op. They also have storage bottles and all manner of other items that would be of interest to an herbalist. Their products are available at many natural food stores and food co-ops throughout the United States. All three of these firms have extremely informative catalogs. Contact information for

Collection and Preparation of Plants

these companies is in the Resources section at the back of this book. There are many other good suppliers out there as well. If you have a computer, search the web.

For the Alchemist growing and collecting their own herbs, collect them at noon when the Sun is highest if the part of the plant to be used is the upper part – leaf, flower, seeds and/or stem. If it is the root of the plant that is needed, then evening is the best time to collect the plant. Ideally, upper plant material is collected on the Full Moon. Plant roots and tubers should be collected on the New Moon.

To follow the planetary days and hours, the Alchemist can choose the day of the week ruled by the planet that also rules the plant, and do so in the hour ruled by that same planet. Another possibility is to also choose a good aspect to the plant's ruling planet and collect when the aspect closes. Or, to keep it simple, just choose the appropriate lunar cycle and time of day without astrological calculations. One can also collect these plants without any of these considerations and still produce a fine elixir. Don't worry about doing any of this "to the t", just enjoy the process and do what you can with the knowledge and resources available to you.

In buying herbs, this same strategy of timing can be applied to the moment of purchase, just as described above for harvesting. Although not necessary, astrological timing can be useful in any endeavor, but one's own intuitions are just as valuable. Essentially if it feels right, then it is time to do whatever task is at hand. We all have astrological clocks within us. Our intuition allows us to access this knowledge if we but meditate upon it and let it manifest.

Herbs that are harvested should be set up to dry immediately. Separate the root from the upper part of the plant.

Herbal Alchemy

Discard the portion not to be used and allow the plant or root to dry for about two weeks, out of direct sunlight in a well ventilated place. Different plants take different times to dry appropriately, and the climate in your area will also make a difference. The point is to drive as much moisture out as possible without applying artificial heat.

For herbs purchased in dried form, the Alchemist need only be concerned with storing them away from excessive humidity, heat and light. The best containers for this purpose are brown glass bottles, or metal canisters with tight lids. These will keep plant material dry, as well as protect it from degradation by light.

Whatever the Alchemist's source of plant material, the next task is to chop or grind each herb very finely into the smallest pieces possible. This creates more extraction surface which speeds the process of extracting the sulphur from the body of the plant. A mortar and pestle, blender and all manner of kitchen tools come in very handy for herbal preparation. Generally it is best to keep plant material as whole as possible in storage and shred or grind it just before extraction. However, some roots become as hard as rocks upon drying. It can be almost impossible to work with them without a fight and some very heavy hammers, so these may be best chopped up before drying. A hydraulic press can overcome this problem and may come in very handy for other operations as well.

The Alchemist's Laboratory

Although it is not necessary, it is ideal for the Alchemist to set aside a room in their home to be used specifically for alchemical operations. The workspace should have a running water supply and a heat source. A workbench with adequate table space and some cabinets to store various items such as herbs, and glassware will be needed. The table top should be covered with some reasonably fireproof material and a small fire extinguisher hung nearby in case of emergency. There should also be some type of exhaust fan to remove the alcohol fumes and the vapors produced by the calcination process. If you have outdoor space available, this is even better as you don't have to worry about fumes accumulating.

That said, it is understood that not every Alchemist is able to have a special room and purchase the ideal equipment to work with. Having all this is not critical for these studies and experiments. Fancy equipment is not the essence of Alchemy, and a few jars along with the proper attitude can be just as effective as all the ritual paraphernalia and equipment imaginable. A suitable spot next to a garden where the herbs are grown and where the Alchemist can draw a magic circle in the earth with a wood fire in the center is also a fine laboratory. For apartment dwellers where space is at a high premium, a simple ritual gesture can call in the appropriate vibration to transform whatever space the Alchemist is using for their ritual operations.

Some Alchemists wear a ring or pendant with a hexagram upon it while doing their work. This hexagram consists of two interlaced triangles, one pointing downward, designat-

Herbal Alchemy

The Hexagram

ing the element of Water, and one pointing upward, for the element of Fire. The hexagram represents balance and cooperation between the great polar opposites. This symbol is worn because the Alchemist works with these elements inwardly as well as in the outer laboratory, and the successful outcome of the process depends on the Alchemist's awareness of these two forces. Although wearing the hexagram is not strictly necessary, it is strongly suggested because it does make a difference. The symbol is a talisman and functions as a psychological reminder. The subtle Feng Shui of such symbols has effects upon the work.

After the Alchemist's laboratory space is set up, a dedication ceremony is performed. The Alchemist ritually cleanses themself as described before when working with the mandala. After the cleansing, the Alchemist proceeds to the lab and puts on the hexagram ring or pendant. As it is put on, the Alchemist meditates on the hexagram and feels that they are perfectly balanced.

The Alchemist's Laboratory

The Alchemist then proceeds to the center of the room and faces east. With eyes closed, they imagine the universal presence entering the room and permeating everything. At this point the Alchemist feels the room, the instruments and they themself are inhabited by the universal presence and that every operation performed will be guided by this principle. At this time the Alchemist also dedicates themself to the great work through their own words and gestures. So that this ritual will have a more personal meaning, it is left up to the individual to choose how to word and gesticulate the ceremony.

It should be mentioned here that every time the Alchemist enters their laboratory at the beginning of any work, they perform the meditation of balance on the hexagram as they put on their ring or pendant. They center themself in the room and realize the universal presence before commencing any operation. It is not necessary to ritually bathe before entering, as is done for the dedication of the laboratory. A simple ritual washing of the hands is sufficient. This symbolic-magical gesture clears the Alchemist's aura of any inharmonious vibrations. Following this ceremony the Alchemist is ready to begin work

After a period of time the Alchemist begins to realize that they are the center of the mandala and the whole world around them is their laboratory, their field of manifest experience. Each moment, movement and environment will reveal its secrets to the Alchemist whether at work or at play. As the Alchemist proceeds further in the process, they will realize that they are the Alchemist, the materia worked upon, the laboratory, and the "essence," all in one.

Salt, Sulphur, And Mercury

As mentioned previously, the alchemical elixir in the herbal kingdom is a mixture of a particular plant's salt, sulphur and mercury. These are the three essentials for every herbal alchemical elixir. The alchemical salt is the calcined ashes of the plant. The sulphur is the oily extract of the plant, and the spirit is the plant's alcohol derived by fermentation. The most ideal way to perform this process is to create the alcohol purely from the plant. However, this makes the process considerably more complicated and drawn out, and thus impractical for most. It is normal practice to add alcohol to extract the spirit, which is the method described in these pages.

The salt represents the body, the sulphur the soul, and the mercury the spirit of the plant. What the herbal Alchemist does is separate these three principles and then unite them again. It is not necessary in the preparation of the elixir to separate the spirit from the soul, so they will be left conjoined to be added to the salt.

The threefold separation is mentioned only for theoretical distinction, as it is not practical, save for a demonstration.

Preparing The Menstruum

A menstruum is simply a term designating the medium through which the essence is extracted from the herb. In alchemical work upon the herbal kingdom this will be either water or alcohol, which represents the penetrating power of the spirit. For any type of extraction, collected dew, spring water, distilled water, grape brandy or grape wine will serve as an excellent menstruum, as is. The stronger the spirit (menstruum) however, the quicker the extraction.

A stronger menstruum can be made by distilling and redistilling the brandy or wine until one obtains the stronger grape alcohol. This is a good menstruum. Other non-poisonous alcohols of about 180 or 190 proof can be obtained at your local spirit shop. Any of these potable alcohols can be strengthened by distillation to get a greater percentage of the water out. This would probably require distilling and redistilling them about seven or eight times. The water will be left in the boiling flask as a residue and should be discarded after each distillation.

To perform the above process, set up a distillation train consisting of the following items: a flask to hold the alcohol, a condenser, a receiver, a thermometer, a two hole rubber or cork stopper, flexible hose to connect to a sink tap and for drainage, stands and clamps to hold the flask and condenser, and a heat source. This equipment can be found at any chemical supply house.

Pour the alcohol into the flask and connect the condenser so that the alcohol will drain into a collection beaker (receiver). The heat should be very gentle as not much is needed for alcohol to evaporate. Alcohol evaporates readily

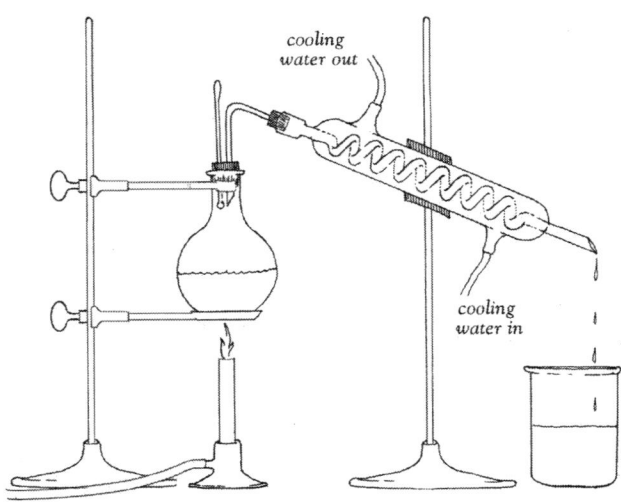

Distillation set-up for preparing the menstruum

at about 79°C (174°F). Water begins to boil at about 100°C (212°F). If the boiling flask has a two hole stopper at the top, insert the thermometer in one hole and the outlet to the condenser in the other. Monitor the thermometer and keep the flame adjusted so that the temperature of the alcohol stays near 79°C. All the alcohol will boil out of the flask, leaving the water behind.

As the alcohol evaporates, it will move through the condenser which is kept cold by a running water supply that comes from your tap and then empties back into the sink. As the alcohol moves through the condenser, it condenses and drips into the beaker. When no more evaporate comes forth, empty the flask and use the alcohol in the beaker, or put it back into the boiling flask to run it through the same cycle. The alcohol will get stronger each time you do this. Preparing the alcohol in this manner will produce a faster acting menstruum, however, it is not necessary. The instructions are

The Alchemist's Laboratory

included here as an aside for those who may be interested. A high school chemistry text will have all the information needed about the distillation process.

Only organic wine, or spirits without any additives should be used. Another way to produce a menstruum is to obtain the spirit (alcohol) of the plant by fermentation. Each plant produces its own peculiar type of alcohol and requires its own particular mix of yeasts, sugars, etc., in order to ferment properly. The process takes extensive experimentation to be able to produce enough alcohol from a plant substance to make it worthwhile. In the process outlined here, we will simply add the spirit rather than produce the alcohol through fermentation.

One can also use morning dew, which makes an excellent menstruum. To collect the dew, lay out cloth upon a lawn during the day, and then at next sunrise, collect the dew by wringing the cloth into a receptacle to hold the water. Dew collected in such a manner should be stored in evaporation tight bottles and used as soon as possible for extraction. Dew is an excellent extractive medium. From an alchemical point of view it has very interesting properties making it useful for a variety of operations.

Bottled spring or distilled water is also a suitable menstruum, but tap water from a municipal water supply is not because it usually contains chemical additives.

Whatever you do – if you use alcohol, use only drinkable, non-poisonous alcohols. Do not use wood alcohol! The Alchemist should also be aware of and implement proper safety precautions in handling, storage, and ventilation when working with alcohol. It should be stressed that all that is really needed is some good fresh water and or good organic wine for a fine menstruum.

Extracting The Herbal Elixir

After preparing the menstruum, the extraction apparatus should be set up. Extraction can be done with anything from a simple jar to the more sophisticated extractors such as a soxhlet. There are many types of extraction devices, available from chemical glassware supply houses. The Alchemist can use a flask extractor, or a boiling flask with a condenser setup on top of it to extract the essence. With these two items, however, you have to put the herb into the flask with the spirit, and this requires filtering after the extraction.

For those who do not want to work with the extraction apparatus, condenser, flask, etc., there is another way that takes a little longer but can still produce a fine elixir. All that is needed for this method is the menstruum and herb, a jar with a lid that has a rubber gasket (canning jars are ideal), a mortar and pestle, wire screen, some filter papers or unbleached natural cheesecloth and a calcining dish. The calcining dish should be a fire resistant dish or pot. It is important not to use glazed pots. Either unglazed clay pots that are heat resistant, or stainless steel or iron is best.

The chosen plant material should be thoroughly dry and reduced to fine particles by chopping or grinding. Be aware that the amount of elixir extracted will be a very tiny percentage of the amount of this plant material, so measure out the herb accordingly. Place the herb in a jar and cover it with brandy or other choice of menstruum. Close the lid on the top of the jar, making sure that it is sealed very well, and put the jar in a warm place to macerate. During maceration the sulphur will be extracted by the spirit (brandy). After a

Extracting the Herbal Elixir

few weeks, pour this extract out and filter the liquid until it is as clear as possible. The essence-depleted body of the plant (the solid matter) is set aside to dry thoroughly.

After the depleted body is fully dry, put it into the calcining dish. Cover the pot or dish with a metal screen and burn the substance to ashes. The screen keeps the burning ashes in the dish. The burning can be done in several ways. A torch can be used, or the pot can be put on a strong fire outside, or inside, if you have a ventilator hood. After a short while the plant material will be turned to ash.

After the pulp is thoroughly burned to ashes, pour the ashes into a mortar and grind them with a pestle. After grinding, put them back into the calcining dish, cover them with the screen, and place the dish over a strong fire to calcine the ashes. As the calcination proceeds the ashes will turn lighter in color. They can be taken out of the dish occasionally and ground with the pestle in the mortar. After a while the ashes will turn a light grey, then white, and after much prolonged calcination, red. For these purposes, a light grey is sufficient, however, the longer the calcination, the better. After prolonged calcination there is only a minute amount of calcined substance left.

The next step is to take the salt (the calcined ashes) and put it into a jar. Pour the liquid extract over the salt and then hermetically seal the jar. Hermetically sealing a jar is simply making sure that it is airtight. If it is not tight, the alcohol or water used will evaporate.

Put the hermetically sealed jar in a warm place (near a heat source) and let the matter digest for a few weeks. Alchemists sometimes use compost piles to provide the heat for this part of the process. If you have a garden and use a fast, hot compost method, the heat of the pile is ideal for

Herbal Alchemy

this process. Just bury the sealed jar in the middle of the pile.

During this time the salt will absorb the essence from the liquid. Simply pour off the liquid, leaving the residue (the salt that has absorbed the essence) in the jar. Seal the jar again and let it sit for another few weeks again in a warm spot. After this, open the container, and let the elixir dry up and granulate. Scrape the dried elixir out of the container and it is ready for use. The elixir can either be stored dry or mixed with alcohol or water in brown glass bottles.

For those with more money to spend, and who wish to speed up the extraction, a soxhlet type of extractor will do the job. This consists of one bulb type condenser, one soxhlet extractor, a thimble, and a flask. Stopcock grease to rub on the connections will also be needed, otherwise the heat could fuse the ground glass connectors which are very fragile. All the apparatus here can be obtained at any chemical supply house. The process is really very simple, but for those not acquainted with the use of extracting apparatus, a high school or college basic chemistry text will be helpful.

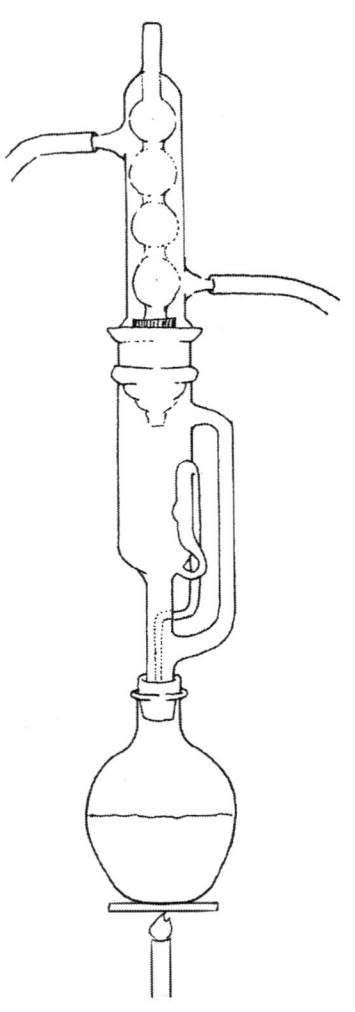

Soxhlet Extractor

Extracting the Herbal Elixir

There should be running water close at hand for the condenser, and a heat source. Place the dried herb in the thimble. Put the thimble into the extractor. Fill the flask with the menstruum to three quarters full and connect it to the extractor. Light the burner, setting it to a moderate flame to avoid scorching the sulphur that is being extracted from the herb. Let the extraction go on for about forty-eight hours. After the extraction is complete, remove the herb and extract from the apparatus. Dry the pulp of the herb, place it in a calcining dish, burn it to ashes, and calcine the ashes, all as described above for the simple extraction methods. The calcined ashes then go into the extractor flask and the extract is poured over them. Put the flask back onto the soxhlet apparatus, turn on the heat and let it circulate for another 48 hours. After this, remove the flask and pour off the extract, leaving the residue (the salt that has absorbed the essence). The flask should be sealed up and set aside near a heat source for one to two weeks, as described in the simple method. Then, open the flask, transfer the elixir to an open jar or tray to dry out. Grind it in a mortar and it is ready for use or storage.

Medicinal Use of the Elixirs

Each herbal elixir has an affinity for various parts of the emotional, mental and physical body according to its astrological rulership. From the alchemical point of view, this means not only that physical disharmonies can be brought to order, but also that various emotional and mental problems can be helped by proper use of the elixirs.

Herbal elixirs are not considered to be cure-alls. According to the Alchemists, they do have properties which can disperse disharmony and balance the nature of our being when applied correctly.

The application of herbal preparations requires common sense and a good understanding of the substances being worked with. The alchemical mode of preparation gives the herbalist another way to advance their knowledge and usefulness as herbal specialists.

The proper administration of dosage is extremely important. A typical dosage would be a few grains of an alchemical elixir in a glass of distilled water. If the problem being treated is very persistent, dosage would be about five to ten grains of the elixir in a glass of distilled water, taken as a teaspoonful every three or four hours every day.

For a general cleansing, the Alchemist prepares an herbal elixir for each of the seven planets and takes each elixir on the day ruled by that planet.

The Alchemist interested in medicinal application of the herbal elixirs should make an in depth study of herbal medicine in order to understand the plant substances and their appropriate administration. As with any other system of

Medicinal Use of the Elixirs

herbal medicine, remember that it is illegal to make claims for any substance which has not been tested and laboratory proven. One can present the claims of the Alchemists and herbalists from a historical perspective, or your own experience or your opinion, but go no further. It is against the law to practice medicine without a license. This is unfortunate for practitioners of the herbal arts.

According to the Alchemists, alchemical elixirs are very effective in their applications, but let them speak for themselves. Make no claims for the elixirs you produce. Anyone is free to state their opinion and relate their experience with herbal applications as is done in this book. However, remember that the herbal arts, no matter what school you follow, are not as widely accepted or understood as they should be for a variety of reasons. Most of these reasons are political and economic. There are vested interests which create resistance to alternative healing practices. Although alternative therapies are slowly being accepted by the powers that be, there is a long way to go before the matter is made right. It is interesting to note that Paracelsus (an Alchemist) is considered the founder of modern medicine and that the caduceus is the symbol that the mainstream healing profession has chosen as its emblem.

Magical Impregnation of the Elixirs

Following the physical preparation of the selected plant the Alchemist impregnates the elixir in a three dimensional alchemical manner. The physical elixir prepared up to this point is the most powerful magical condenser that can be made from the vegetable kingdom. A magical condenser is a substance which has an enhanced capacity to hold energy, vibrations, thought forms, etc., by virtue of its constituents and/or preparation (such as an alchemical elixir). It is possible to impress upon or impregnate any substance or object with a thought or a feeling. However, not every substance has the same capacity to maintain that form, thought or feeling, nor is every thought compatible with every substance. It happens that some substances dampen the impregnation slowly to the point where it becomes extinct. That is why certain plants are used for specific purposes. Also, before proceeding with the practice of impregnating the elixirs, it is important that you spend some time meditating on two very important axioms:

What is here is there, what is not here is not there.
(Visvasara Tantra)

As above so below, as within so without
(Emerald Tablet of Hermes)

Each of these phrases means the same thing, which is, put most simply, that in every object, thought or atom, etc., is contained the whole universe. In other words, every object contains all other objects. The Alchemist realizing this through meditation, also knows that although everything in the universe is contained within any object, any specific

Magical Impregnation of the Elixirs

object emanates more strongly on one wavelength than on others. A wooden chair, for example, could not exist if it did not have all seven planetary functions within it, but it vibrates at the Saturn frequency more so than a glass of water, which emanates a lunar vibration. That is why some herbs are used for jupiterian purposes, for instance, and others for venusian.

In the beginning of the book it was said that a certain elixir, plant, etc., has the same vibratory rate as the planet that rules it. The Alchemist goes one step further, and actually says that the plant itself is the planet. To illustrate this principle, take a piece of wire and bend it to a "u" shape. Now, poke both ends of the wire through a piece of paper. On a certain plane of perception it appears that there are two objects jutting up at different points, but if viewed from underneath, it can be seen that the wire is actually one piece and not two.

To some this may seem a rather silly example, however, in the late 1990s, experiments in quantum physics confirmed the fact that all materia has a quantum connection, which fully coincides with the above demonstration.

When the first edition of this book was written in 1973-74, it was a struggle to try to present these various time-space concepts so that the reader could easily understand them. Now, with the dissemination of the results of quantum experiments, it is an easy matter to refer the skeptics to the appropriate literature. Einstein himself at one time called quantum mechanics, "Spooky action at a distance." Science is slowly catching up to the mystic, magician and Alchemist. Most quantum physicists will honestly admit that the strange reality of the quantum level is very real, but that in fact they do not really understand why.

Herbal Alchemy

The Alchemist should meditate on what has been said thus far and try to get a clear conceptual picture of this unity-multiplicity dynamic.

Practice I

Alchemical tradition posits three major divisions or dimensions of existence. These three dimensions of time and space have always have been a part of occult lore. In some spiritual traditions, these major three have been divided up into a myriad of levels.

Any region can be divided and subdivided into as many sub-regions as necessary to explain the geography and customs of a place. For instance, to be descriptive in a general way one can say, "This is the planet Earth" or we can say "Los Angeles on the planet Earth." Despite the fact that, for instance, Ireland and Mongolia are on the same planet, from one perspective they have vastly different characteristics. From another perspective they are similar in that they share the characteristics inherent with being a location on the planet Earth.

Each spiritual tradition has either a very simple general description of different dimensions of time and space such as over there, the next world, summerland, valhalla, heaven, etc.; or a complex hierarchy of divisions, such as the Tantric lokas. Most modern day magician-Alchemist-mystics refer to these other dimensions in three divisions: the mental, astral, and physical planes. Each plane is a discrete dimension in time and space but is interdependent with all other dimensions.

The physical plane is what we see about us. It is the whole dimension of time and space in the physical world as we perceive it. The astral plane is a dimension of time and space with a higher vibratory rate than the physical plane.

Magical Impregnation of the Elixirs

The mental plane has a higher vibratory rate than either the physical or astral. Although these dimensions of time and space share the same location, they can be visualized as layers arranged according to hierarchy of vibratory rate, with the mental plane on top, above the astral plane, and both of these above the physical plane. These planes can be divided further into layers, regions and spheres.

The Quabbalists divide space-time into four basic layers or worlds with a hierarchy of sephira (spheres). Vedic based traditions generally prefer 49 divisions (one division for each bead on the necklace of Kali). It should be discerned that, although given different names and divided in many different ways, the "other world" and dimensions of time and space described by different traditions all refer to the same thing.

Various mystics also perceive in many different ways according to their upbringing and training. The substances of these other dimensions of time and space are very pliable and to a certain extent take shape from our preconceived notions. Remember here that quantum physics states that the observer affects the results observed! For instance, a comparison of near-death experiences recorded from various cultures with different religious persuasions will usually show a great deal of cultural evocation. A Christian, for example, will see Christ; a Buddhist will see Buddha; a Moslem a figure of Mohammed, and so on. The principle is the same – guidance, nurturing, help – but the form is different.

This leads to another alchemical axiom which is rather tongue and cheek: What you believe is exactly what you will get. This holds true at least on the lower astral where our dream life occurs and many of the created thought forms of religions reside. As a matter of fact, many esoteric systems use forms such as angels, demons, devas, spirits and intel-

Herbal Alchemy

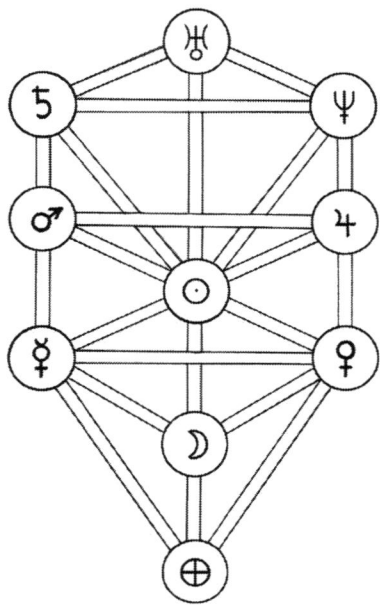

Quabbalistic Tree of Life

ligences as aids to communicate and discern various levels of energy. It is a convenient device and works quite well as humans have a tendency to anthropomorphize everything.

In the Quabbala system, for example, many mantras are related to such forms (angels, archangels, gods or goddesses) for each sphere. These are symbolic names and structures for a particular group of forces with particular characteristics. It is not necessary to conceptualize these forces as angels with wings as popular mythology renders them, but one can do so if one chooses. The point is that there are many characterizations of the various energies of the universe and many ways to order them, but all of us are working with the same substance and same dimensions. How anyone chooses to characterize and see and feel their way through the cosmos is entirely up to them, according to their lights.

Magical Impregnation of the Elixirs

According to alchemical tradition, manifestation proceeds from the inner to the outer. Formation proceeds down through the planes (dimensions) from the causal through the mental and the astral down through to the physical plane. The five elements are present on each plane and are the building blocks of all form and force on all these planes of perception. Alchemists, although talking mostly in terms of three (mental, astral, and physical), really work consciously with five subdivisions of materia – causal, mental, astral, etheric and physical – as represented by the pentagram and pentagrammaton . The pentagrammaton is related to Fire and is the first and foremost tool for the Alchemist.

There are several different ways to approach the magical impregnation of the elixirs. To perform this task, one can skip consideration, for instance, of the causal plane as that impetus is already active. This is because the magician-Alchemist is involved in the process, that is, the magician-Alchemist's intent to impregnate the elixir is the causal sphere impetus. But formation in the mental, astral and physical spheres is required for the elixir to be earthed. Again, the etheric plane can be treated the same as the physical representation of the elixir, because the physical elixir has an etheric counterpart and is already vibrating strongly the elixir's planetary frequency.

On the other hand, the causal and etheric planes can be considered and worked with consciously and directly to set in the impregnation most firmly. There is more than one way to accomplish the same task. What is presented here are only the most meagre guidelines, but from this explanation, the Alchemist should be able to apply whatever system they are working with to the task of magical impregnation of the elixirs in an alchemical manner.

Herbal Alchemy

One mode of impregnation is as follows: let's say the Alchemist has prepared a Jupiter elixir for a specific purpose. They should put the elixir before themselves, close their eyes, and transfer their consciousness into the substance. At the time of transfer they must realize that this substance is the Jupiter sphere, and that in this state the Alchemist's whole being, while in the elixir, is actually in the mental, astral, and physical sphere of that planet.

The Alchemist must feel and know that the elixir and the planet are one. At this point the Alchemist impregnates the physical body of the substance with the purpose intended. The Alchemist then impregnates the astral body of the elixir with the same purpose and finally the mental body. If the Alchemist has prepared an aspected elixir, they proceed as usual impregnating all three spheres with their intention, but with the idea in mind that the elixir is the planet in aspect.

Another mode of magical impregnation is in the western Quabbalistic manner. The use of certain words of power coupled with a color scheme is the most dominant factor here. If you wish to study further in this regard Franz Bardon's book The Key To The True Quabbalah is a good resource, as well as other texts listed in the bibliography. Each planetary sephira on the Tree of Life manifests on four planes: Atziluth, Briah, Yetzirah, Assiah. Atziluth is the causal, Briah is the mental plane, Yetzirh is the astral plane, and Assiah is the physical plane. There is a color and sound value for each of the sephira on each of the four planes.

Practice II

The Alchemist first constructs an earthing disk, called a pentacle. This disk represents the four elements and their working on the physical plane, and is a kind of magical lightening rod or conductor. It becomes a focal point for the evoked forces.

Magical Impregnation of the Elixirs

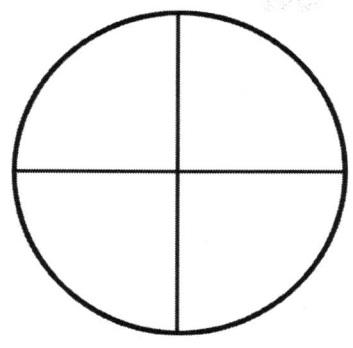

The Pentacle is a simple disk with crosscuts dividing it into four sections, each representing one of the four elements. The disk can be constructed of clay. The quarters can be painted with red for Fire, light blue for Air, green for Water, and yellow-ochre for Earth.

Planetary plates are also constructed, and when any particular planet is in use, its plate should be placed upon the pentacle. Specifics for making the plates are in each planet's section on the following pages. During the magical impregnation, the elixir is put upon the planetary plate. For example, if the Alchemist wishes to impregnate a Jupiter elixir, they set the pentacle before them. On top of this is placed a plate with the planetary seal for Jupiter, then the elixir is placed on the seal. Two candles should be put on either side of the disk and should be lit.

The Alchemist then takes a meditative posture before the elixir, and transfers their consciousness into the elixir, at the same time realizing that they are transferring themselves into the causal sphere of the planet. The Alchemist visualizes the causal color for that sphere, which in this case is deep violet. They feel immersed in, and surrounded by the deep violet of the Jupiter sphere in the causal. At this point they silently charge the elixir with their purpose by the divine name and power of El. The Alchemist then transfers their consciousness into the mental sphere of the elixir, which is blue. When the Alchemist feels comfortably situated in the mental sphere of the sephira, they continue by silently charging Tzadqiel with

Herbal Alchemy

the task of impregnating the elixir with their desire under the divine presidency of El. The Alchemist then proceeds to the astral sphere of the elixir which in this case is deep purple and proceeds to charge the Chasmalim in a whispering voice with the task of impregnating the elixir with the task at hand under the presidency of El and in the name of Tzadqiel.

The next step is for the Alchemist to transfer their consciousness into the etheric-physical sphere of the elixir. Here the color will be a deep azure flecked with yellow. In a loud voice the Alchemist charges this sphere of Tzedek with their desire under the presidency of El and in the name of Tzadqiel by the power of the Chasmalim. Next is to charge Sachiel with the task of impregnating the elixir under the presidency of El, in the name of Tzadqiel, by the power of the Chasmalim, and by divine order of Sachiel in the sphere of Tzedek. Then, Hismael is charged with the task of impregnating the elixir under the presidency of El, by the name Tzadqiel, by the power of the Chasmalim, by the divine order of Sachiel, and Iophiel. Finally, the Alchemist then charges the four elements with the task of impregnating the elixir under the presidency of El, in the name of Tzadqiel, by the power of the Chasmalim, by divine order of Sachiel, Iophiel and Hismael, in the sphere of Tzedek "the elixir"

After the ritual the Alchemist puts the elixir away, blows out the candles and covers the planetary plate and pentacle in silk cloth.

If you are acquainted with the practice of meditation you will find this technique easy to work with, Each name is a mantra which is coupled with its yantra (sigil or mandala) and color, to produce a connection with the sphere involved. The technique basically remains the same in all esoteric systems. The sound values, mantras, color schemes, and so

Magical Impregnation of the Elixirs

forth may be different, but the general mode of operation is consistent.

Notice that this process engages both right brain (color, geometrical shapes, and sound) as well as left brain (thought and language). Of course, it is possible to impregnate the elixirs without the use of divine names. However, the connection with these names lifts the Alchemist out of the individual human sphere of limited capabilities, and helps the Alchemist to combine with the energy in its unhindered form. It actually allows a quick focussing of powers that might otherwise be inhibited by the various psychological complexes residing in the Alchemist's mental, astral or physical bodies. Thus the appeal to seemingly outside forces, or representations of those outside forces, is really an aid for producing the phenomenon.

All of these forces reside within us, and indeed, they are us. However, the attitude and stance in the ritual elaborated above will help the Alchemist to use the full vibration of these forces, unrestricted by personal psychological limitations. Humans tend to perceive themselves as what they seem to be at the moment, thus their powers are limited by what they perceive to be their gifts and skills, and they manifest only a very small portion of their potential at any given point in time.

To realize a fuller potential, the Alchemist uses a ritual stance such as the one detailed above, to move out of and beyond their limited perception of themself. Even with the intellectual understanding that each of us is all the universe, it is simply book knowledge and must be put into practice by combining the various elements on all planes – mental, astral, physical – for the fuller potential to manifest. This takes some understanding and work. The application of these techniques, even if not understood initially, will gently bring the Alchemist to a realization of their own hidden capabilities.

Any system will work to impregnate the elixirs, even a system made up by the Alchemist. The closer the symbols are to the correct analogies, and to the Alchemist's karma, the more comfortable they will be to work with. The main purpose of this text is to present an example of the ways that an Alchemist can perform certain operations.

The realities of time and space, as quantum physics is beginning to discover, are not what we have thought they were. The comfortable simple world that we perceive around us is only supported by agreement. The observer affects the outcome. Group karma affects us greatly. Humans are raised with certain beliefs, and as a result, other avenues and connections are shut down and hidden from them. This is the action of the Saturn sphere karma (muladhara chakra). Thus, the Alchemist separates what is before them, reduces matter to its constituents, and then recombines them. It is not only a physical process, but a mental and emotional-feeling process that the Alchemist engages in to discern the reality behind the illusion that is perceived as real by most of humanity.

It is important to remember when using these techniques that the use of divine names, etc. should not be confused with any religious connotation wherein deities are placated by various actions, observances, behaviors, etc. To put it in a nutshell: if you see an Alchemist praying to god, you can assume they are praying to themselves, to that part of themselves that they desire to connect with, in order to complete the task at hand. The Alchemist thus understands that they themself are the beginning and end of all things.

Quabbalistic Values for the Planetary Spheres

Sounds, colors, sigils, and geometric shapes from the Quabbalistic tradition are used in Alchemy to tune in to the various planes and spheres that represent the task at hand. These symbols are tools to link the Alchemist with the time-space segments that represent the vibration that the Alchemist wishes to connect with.

There are many different approaches even within the Quabbalistic school of thought, but they all go to the same places. To truly understand the science behind the total mythology-theology of these sounds, colors and geometric symbols would take many years of left brain study as there are many thousands of years of cultural synthesis involved and integrated into each value.

However, years of intense study are not necessary to understand enough to utilize these tools. Sound, color and geometry emit vibrations of a frequency that resonate and match particular forces and forms, whatever their plane (dimension) of existence. By simply having these tools in the environment, the Alchemist will begin to resonate with the sphere involved. Human consciousness is shaped by what is in our field of perception, or, in other words, what's placed in front of our noses. Looking at a teapot actually transforms your mind substance into the teapot. You are not simply seeing a teapot – you become that teapot, and that is why you see it. There are many secrets veiled within even the most common perceptions, which upon reflection, will offer many interesting avenues for study.

Herbal Alchemy

Sets of colors, sounds, and shapes are really energy level transmutation or transformation points. They are keys or links to and through various levels of vibration which comprise the great sea of energy within which we move and have our being. Such terms as god, archangel, angel, etc., to the initiate merely designate a hierarchy of movement or operation, and have nothing to do with popular theology.

For example, if a person wants to go somewhere in a car, they must do certain things in a certain order and with certain parts of the car itself. One must first open the door and get in, and have a key that fits the ignition lock. The key is then inserted, which makes the engine run, and then the transmission must be engaged, and so forth. Each of these things must be done in a specific order, other-wise the car simply won't take you where you want to go.

So, although the use of such designations as angels and hierarchies may seem silly, go deeper into what it is that is really being conveyed before making a judgement. What seems to be theological folderol may intentionally hide many secrets of occult operations.

By simply using these tools, one can tune in to the sphere involved and thus connect with the knowledge and experience contained within that sphere. Again, there are many secrets hidden in the methodology presented, and only practice will reveal these mysteries. For a deeper understanding of this methodology, Franz Bardon's book, *The Key to The True Quabbalah* is a good resource for further study.

It should be noted that there are no traditional seals for Neptune, Uranus and Pluto, which is why they will not be found in the following pages. The astrological symbols for Uranus and Neptune can be used to make plates for those planetary spheres.

Quabbalistic Values for the Planetary Spheres

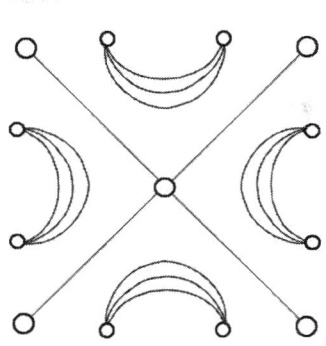

*The Seal of the Moon
should be etched on silver. If painted
it should be done in a cream color.*

Yesod, the Sphere of the Moon

Sounds

Causal	Shaddai El Chai, God
Mental	Gabriel, Archangel
Astral	Kerubim, Angels
Physical	The Sphere of the Moon on the physical plane is called Levanah
Angel	Gabriel
Intelligence	Malkah Be Tarshisim Ve Ad Ruachoth Schechalim
Spirit	Shad Barshemoth Ha Shartathan

Colors

Physical	citron with undertones of azure
Astral	very dark purple
Mental	violet
Causal	indigo

Herbal Alchemy

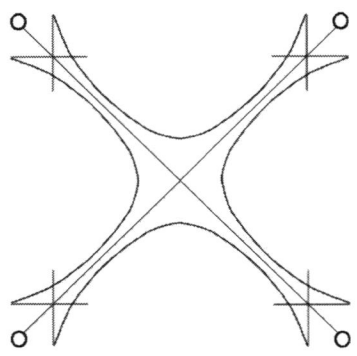

*The Seal of the Sun
should be etched on gold. If painted
it should be done in gold color.*

Tiphareth, the Sphere of the Sun

Sounds

Causal	YHVH Eloah Ve Daath, God
Mental	Raphael, Archangel
Astral	Melechim, Angels
Physical	The Sphere of the Sun on the physical plane is called Shemesh
Angel	Michael
Intelligence	Nachiel
Spirit	Sorath

Colors

Physical	gold amber
Astral	rich salmon
Mental	yellow/gold
Causal	clear pink rose

Quabbalistic Values for the Planetary Spheres

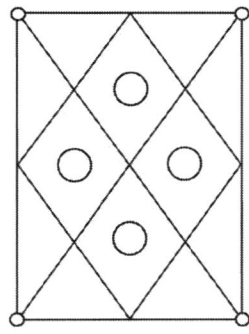

*The Seal of Mercury
should be etched in brass. If painted
it should be done in silver.*

Hod, the Sphere of Mercury

Sounds

Causal	Elohim Tzabaoth, God
Mental	Michael, Archangel
Astral	Beni Elohim, Angels
Physical	The Sphere of Mercury on the physical plane is called Kokab
Angel	Raphael
Intelligence	Tiriel
Spirit	Taphthartharath

Colors

Physical	yellow brown with undertones of white
Astral	red russet
Mental	orange
Causal	violet/purple

Herbal Alchemy

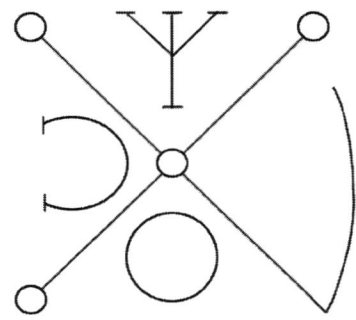

*The Seal of Venus
should be done in copper. If painted
it should be done in green.*

Netzach, the Sphere of Venus

Sounds

Causal	YHVH Tzabaoth, God
Mental	Haniel, Archangel
Astral	Elohim, Angels
Physical	The Sphere of Venus on the physical plane is called Nogah
Angel	Hanael
Intelligence	Hagiel
Spirit	Kedemel

Colors

Physical	olive with undertones of gold
Astral	bright yellow green
Mental	emerald
Causal	amber

Quabbalistic Values for the Planetary Spheres

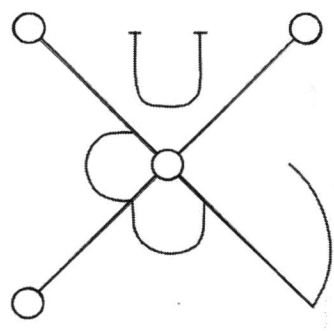

*The Seal of Mars
should be etched on iron or steel. If painted
it should be done in red.*

Geburah, the Sphere of Mars

Sounds

Causal	Elohim, Gibor, God
Mental	Kamael, Archangel
Astral	Seraphim, Angels
Physical	The Sphere of Mars on the physical plane is called Madim
Angel	Zamael
Intelligence	Graphiel
Spirit	Bartzabel

Colors

Physical	red with undertones of black
Astral	bright scarlet
Mental	scarlet red
Causal	orange

Herbal Alchemy

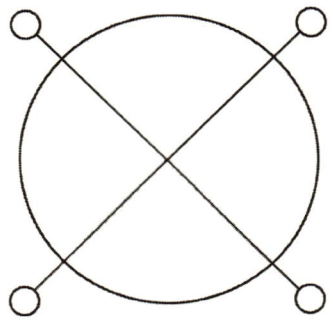

The Seal of Jupiter should be etched on tin. If painted it should be done in blue.

Chesed, the Sphere of Jupiter

Sounds

Causal	El, God
Mental	Tzadqiel, Archangel
Astral	Chashmalim, Angels
Physical	The Sphere of Jupiter on the physical plane is called Tzedek
Angel	Sachiel
Intelligence	Iophiel
Spirit	Hismael

Colors

Physical	deep azure with undertones of yellow
Astral	deep purple
Mental	blue
Causal	deep violet

Quabbalistic Values for the Planetary Spheres

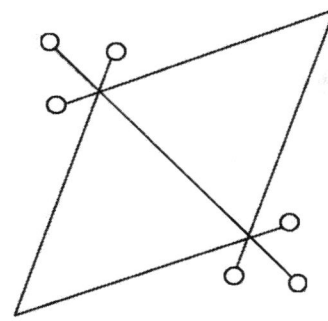

*The Seal of Saturn,
should be etched on lead. If painted,
it should be done in black.*

Binah, the Sphere of Saturn

Sounds

Causal	IHVH Elohim, God
Mental	Tzaphqiel, Archangel
Astral	Aralim, Angels
Physical	The Sphere of Saturn on the physical plane is called Shabbathai
Angel	Cassiel
Intelligence	Agiel
Spirit	Zazel

Colors

Physical	grey with undertones of pink
Astral	dark brown
Mental	black
Causal	crimson

Solve et Coagula

Solve et coagula is one of the grand formulas of Alchemy. Dissolve and coalesce, break down and build up. The formula is at once simple, and yet complex. It is both the Alchemist's best friend and greatest enemy. It is the great work of the Alchemist as well as the great work of the Grand Alchemist. In all cosmic processes this grand formula will be found at work. Loosely considered, in the Hindu pantheon, *solve* is Shiva the destroyer, and *coagula* is Vishnu the preserver.

In more personal terms, this formula represents the constant dissolution and restructuring of the ego that the Alchemist must go through on the way to universal consciousness. As understanding and wisdom grows, new psychological structures are needed. Old views and prejudices which block the influx of universal wisdom must be cast out to make way for a new, more centered consciousness. The astrological keywords for Pluto (which is the ruling planet of Alchemy and psychoanalysis) express this process quite succinctly: elimination, renewal, regeneration. Here is the key to the exoteric meaning of baptism, the concept of rebirth and the function of Anubis in the Egyptian pantheon. This plutonian formula is the result of basic action and interaction on the different parts of the circle-point mandala, which is in constant motion, causing the myriad of observable phenomena which surrounds us. The last dissolution and restructuring is the result of perfect centering and represents the Brahmin formula *Aum*, which is the matrix for all manifestation in what we would call the universal ego.

The Alchemist sees all manifestation as the representation of this universal ego, and all the processes and objects

Solve et Coagula

within this manifested ego are a part of the psychology of the universal spirit.

The dynamics of this manifest consciousness, which is simply movement in space (vibration) is the psychology of Alchemy. A thought, a human interaction, a tree and its growth cycle through time, the orbital motion of the Earth, as well as the birth and death of a star are all the results of this spirit's ideation or psychology of manifest experience.

This includes the Alchemist themself. As you move through your journey of discovery, you will realize that your personality is only a partial representation of the total experience of universal consciousness. Due to natural inclination, you will move closer to the center to satisfy a sense of discovery, which is in essence a manifestation of the universal spirit's intense desire to transcend its own space-time continuum. As your movement towards the center progresses you will become more aware of the *Om Ahum Brahma Smi* formula of Tantric yoga. This mantric formula simply means "I am the Creator" and it is this goal to which all students of the arcane sciences must aspire.

Resources for Further Study

Magical texts

There are many authors who provide the magical background material needed for the study of Alchemy. Among these are Franz Bardon, Israel Regardie, Arthur Avalon, Dion Fortune, Mary Anne Atwood, and many others.

Franz Bardon's three volume introduction into magical science is highly recommended. At the very least, procure the first volume of the series, *Initiation into Hermetics*, which is a very nuts and bolts introduction into the practice of magic. Dion Fortune's *Mystical Qabalah* is an easily understood, definitive guide to quabbalistic magic. Israel Regardie's *The Middle Pillar* and *The Complete Golden Dawn System of Magic* offers great insight into the practice of magical ritual and the importance of psychological analysis of self as one progresses as an Alchemist and magician. There are also other texts by these authors that are of great value in the study of Alchemy.

Bardon, Franz
Initiation Into Hermetics
Wuppertal, West Germany: Dieter Ruggeberg, 1976

Bardon, Franz
The Key To The True Quabbalah
Wuppertal, West Germany: Dieter Ruggeberg, 1975

Regardie, Israel,
The Middle Pillar
Saint Paul, MN: Llewellyn, 1970

Regardie, Israel
The Complete Golden Dawn System of Magic
Scottsdale, AZ: New Falcon Publications, 1990

Resources for Further Study

Fortune, Dion
The Mystical Qabalah
New York, NY: Alta Gaia Books, 1979

Atwood, Mary Anne
A Suggestive Inquiry into Hermetic Mystery
London, William Tait, 1918

Avalon, Arthur
The Serpent Power
New York, NY: Dover Publications, 1974

Psychology

Any works by Carl Jung will be of value. Although Jung never claimed to be an Alchemist, his interpretations of alchemical texts were highly influential in his development of a viable system of psychoanalysis. Jung also did astrological natal charts of his patients. Certain of his texts are more rewarding than others, but all have Alchemy as a main thread, and they are quite enlightening from a psychological point of view.

Synthesis

The writings of R. A. Schwaller De Lubicz are highly recommended. De Lubicz spent many years in Egypt deciphering the underlying structure of ancient Egyptian hieroglyphs as they relate to space-time contexts, and thus magic. A good introduction to De Lubicz's work is *Serpent in the Sky* by John Anthony West.

Morning of the Magicians by Louis Pauwels and Jacques Bergier is enlightening and quite fascinating to read as they raise several important points about magic, Alchemy and science. *The Tao of Physics* by Fritjof Capra is a classic that bridges the gap between magic and mysticism, and present day quantum physics. It addresses any doubts you may have about the reality behind Alchemy and magic. Any books by Mircea Eliade will put into perspective the many culturally diverse ways humankind has developed and ritualized their inner knowledge. Michel Gauquelin's *The Cosmic Clocks: From Astrology to a Modern Science* is a great introduction to the synthesis of Astrology and scientific understanding. Louis Kervran's *Biological Transmutations* offers interesting insights into the Alchemy of everyday biological processes

West, Anthony, John
Serpent in the Sky
New York, NY: Julian Press, 1987

De Lubicz, Schwaller, R. A.
The Symbol and the Symbolic
Cairo, Egypt: Le Caire, 1957

Eliade, Mircea
The Forge and the Crucible:
The Origins and Structures of Alchemy
Chicago: University of Chicago Press, 1979

Eliade, Mircea
The Sacred & the Profane: the Nature of Religion
New York: NY, Harcourt Brace, 1957

Pauwels, Louis, and Jacques Bergier
The Morning of the Magicians
New York, NY: Avon Books, 1968

Capra, Fritjof
The Tao of Physics
Shambhala Publications, 1977

Resources for Further Study

Kervran, Louis
Biological Transmutations
Brooklyn, NY: Swan House Publishing, 1973

Gauquelin, Michel
The Cosmic Clocks: From Astrology to a Modern Science
Chicago, IL: Henry Regnery, 1967

Astrology

Both the *Astrologers Handbook* and *Predictive Astrology* by Frances Sakoian, and Louis Acker give a good background of planetary aspects and their meanings as well as other fundamentals of astrology that are helpful in understanding Alchemy. Nicholas Culpepper's classic 17th century work *Culpepper's Complete Herbal* will provide some background in astrological rulerships as they relate to the plant kingdom.

Sakoian, Frances, and Louis S. Acker
The Astrologers Handbook
New York, NY: Harper & Row, 1987

Sakoian, Frances, and Louis S. Acker
Predictive Astrology
New York, NY: Harper & Row, 1987

Culpepper, Nicholas
Culpepper's Complete Herbal
Great Britain: W. Foulsham & Co. Ltd. 1826

Herbal Alchemy

Physical Preparation of the Herbal Alchemical Elixirs

Albert Riedel's (Frater Albertus) work *The Alchemist's Handbook* is a very good introduction of the physical aspects of the laboratory method used to produce basic herbal elixirs and the vegetable stone.

Albertus, Frater
The Alchemist's Handbook
York Beach, ME: Samuel Weiser, 1987

Alchemy in General

The writings of Basil Valentine and Paracelsus are classic texts of Western Alchemy. There are many other thousands of old and new books about Alchemy from many traditions – Ayurvedic, Taoist, and Tantric, as well as the European – and there are many pearls of wisdom to be culled from them.

Sources for Plant Material

Richter's Herbs
Goodwood, Ontario Canada LOC 1AO
www. richters. com

Seeds, plants, dried herbs, books, seminars.
Huge selection, and excellent information available both in their catalog and on their website.

J. L Hudson, Seedsman
Star Route 2, Box 337
La Honda CA 94020 USA
www. jlhudsonseeds. net

Large selection of seeds of all sorts, and an extremely informative catalog.

Resources for Further Study

Frontier Natural Products Co-op
3021 78th St.
PO Box 299
Norway IA 52318 USA
www.frontiercoop.com

Large selection of dried herbs, herbal products, and tools for the herbalist.

Suggested Herbal References

Grieve, Maude
A Modern Herbal
New York, NY: Dover Publications, 1982

Millspaugh, Charles
American Medicinal Plants
New York, NY: Dover Publications, 1974

Sturtevant, Lewis, (U. P. Hedrick, ed.)
Sturtevant's Edible Plants of the World
New York, NY: Dover Publications, 1976

Tantra, Yoga of Ecstasy:
the Sadhaka's Guide to Kundalini and the Left-Hand Path

by Leigh Hurley & Phillip Hurley

Tantra is an ancient discipline with deep cosmic roots. Every movement in time and space is ritual for the Tantric sadhaka, and every moment is a moment of transmutation, of alchemy. Shiva and Shakti bring us back to first principles in a feeling way that engages all of our senses, and all levels of our being. The Tantric sadhaka is enlightened by the manifestation of these first principles in their life - physically, psychologically, sociologically, and spiritually.

Tantra, Yoga of Ecstasy details ritual, practice, meditation and psychology for the serious student of Tantra.

Topics discussed include:

- ॐ Meaning and intent of classical Tantric rituals
- ॐ Tantric philosophy
- ॐ How to raise kundalini
- ॐ Shiva-Shakti meditation and Tantric initiation
- ॐ Tantra, art & creativity
- ॐ Alchemy of personal transmutation
- ॐ Deciphering the puzzle of Tantric morality
- ॐ Tantric use of astrology

www.tantrayoga.us

Namarupa:
the Magic of Tantra Mantra

by Phillip Hurley & Leigh Hurley

Namarupa is an initiation into mantra yoga, complete with detailed Sanskrit pronunciation, alphabet and calligraphy guides. All mantras are presented in Devanagari script with English transliteration for easy reference. Written from the perspective of the tantric sadhaka (practitioner), Namarupa presents the esoteric meanings and uses of the mantras and alphabet; and discusses mantra sadhana both as classically practiced and updated for modern life. Of special interest are detailed Tantric mantra techniques for raising kundalini, previously available only to initiates.

Namarupa: the Magic of Tantra Mantra includes:

- ॐ Sanskrit letter portraits
- ॐ Sanskrit quick reference tables & pronunciation guide
- ॐ How to initiate a mantra
- ॐ Japa, pranayama, and modes of chanting
- ॐ Detailed discussion of bija mantras
- ॐ Timing & rectification of mantras
- ॐ Deity, planetary, directional & general mantras
- ॐ Mantra cycles for working with the five elements and raising kundalini
- ॐ Likhita japa and calligraphy guides

www.tantrayoga.us

Kundalini:
Tantra Yoga in Practice

by Phillip Hurley & Leigh Hurley

This is an approachable, lucid and engaging guide to the philosophy of Tantra, and its techniques for raising kundalini. The authors have many years experience in spiritual practice and study as initiates under the direct guidance of Goswami Kriyananda, in the lineage of Shellji and his guru, Paramahansa Yogananda.

Kundalini: Tantra Yoga in Practice is a workbook with a wide range of clearly detailed and illustrated techniques for developing an effective personal kundalini practice. It is suitable for beginners, and as a class guide for Hatha Yoga teachers who wish to introduce and integrate kundalini meditation into their offerings.

Presented here are down-to-earth methods based on classical Tantric tradition and agamas. Includes:

- ॐ What is Kundalini?
- ॐ Raising Kundalini
- ॐ The Subtle Anatomy of Kundalini
- ॐ Svantantrya
- ॐ Karma and Maya
- ॐ Prepatory Practices
- ॐ Lifestyle Suggestions
- ॐ Yoga Nidra
- ॐ Tribindu Pranayama
- ॐ Working with Chakras
- ॐ Vajra Vidyut
- ॐ Upavestana
- ॐ Yajna
- ॐ Siddhis, Astrology and Kundalini

www.tantrayoga.us

Once Upon a Yogi Time: Tales of the Siddhis

by Phillip Hurley

What happens when an average person takes up the practice of yoga and begins to experience the siddhis - the paranormal abilities of yogi legend?

These are true stories of a modern western yogi's light-hearted personal journey into the realms of magic and mysticism. The path to cosmic consciousness sometimes winds through a maze of extraordinary phenomena: mischievous ghosts, astral projection, devas and geniis, materialization, psychokinesis, astrology and remote viewing, to name a few. Guided by a recalcitrant guru and driven by his own insatiable curiosity, adjusting to living with siddhis results in some eye-opening and often humorous moments.

www.tantrayoga.us

Made in the USA
Monee, IL
05 November 2020